W9-AVK-658

Arizona's Historic Restaurants and Their Recipes

Arizona's Historic Restaurants and Their Recipes

by Karen Surina Mulford

Drawings by

Patsy Faires

and Debra Long Hampton

John F. Blair, Publisher
Winston-Salem, North Carolina

Copyright © 1995 by John F. Blair, Publisher

Printed in the United States of America

All Rights Reserved

DESIGN BY DEBRA LONG HAMPTON

MAP BY LIZA LANGRALL

PHOTOGRAPH ON FRONT COVER BY TIM FULLER

PHOTOGRAPH ON BACK COVER BY GREY CRAWFORD

PRINTED AND BOUND BY R. R. DONNELLEY & SONS

Library of Congress Cataloging-in-Publication Data

Mulford, Karen.

Arizona's historic restaurants and their recipes / Karen Mulford.

p.   cm.

Includes index.

ISBN 0-89587-132-7 (alk. paper)

1. Cookery—Arizona.   2. Restaurants—Arizona—Guidebooks.

3. Historic buildings—Arizona.   I. Title.

TX715.M9287   1995

641.59791—dc20   95-32834

Foreword

$\mathcal{A}$rizona's history is written on her landscape, an incredible panorama which stretches across great canyons and painted deserts, mountain peaks, and pine forests. Arizona's very name excites the imagination with scenes of the Old West—of cowboys and Indians, gunslingers and cattle rustlers, careening stagecoaches and dusty mining camps. It is a land as ancient and diverse as the people who claimed it and shaped her rich heritage, beginning with prehistoric Hohokam and Anasazi Indians, and followed by Spanish explorers, missionaries from Mexico, pioneer miners, cowboys, cattlemen, and courageous women. Through Arizona's long history, as new settlers arrived, towns and cities began to emerge across the landscape. Some failed the test of time and became ghost towns. Others survived and prospered. Today, these towns contain interesting historic structures that provide a unique glimpse into Arizona's colorful past.

As I traveled Arizona's backroads and highways in search of fifty historic restaurants, I was often reminded of an old saying: "When the student is ready, the teacher appears." Even though I was an experienced traveler familiar with Arizona's interesting landscape, I felt like an enthusiastic student, thrilled with a chance to explore once again the state where I was raised and attended school. And since I believe that much can be learned about a state by visiting its historic structures, each aged building I discovered became a wonderful teacher, rich with lessons of Arizona's history.

The restaurants that appear in this book are housed in historic buildings as diverse and interesting as Arizona's extraordinary terrain. From a window seat in the rustic dining rooms of the Grand Canyon's Bright Angel Lodge and elegant, world-famous El Tovar Hotel, I enjoyed breathtaking views of the canyon's incredible south rim. At the posh Orangerie in the luxurious Arizona Biltmore Resort in Phoenix, I dined on exquisite, contemporary French cuisine and marveled at the structure's distinctive pre-cast concrete blocks, inspired by architect Frank Lloyd Wright and molded on the site in 1929. In Tombstone, the country's best-known Western town, I was served lunch in a century-old restaurant located around the corner from the OK Corral—the site of the famous gunfight that is still re-enacted regularly, preserving the town's notorious "Wild West" image. In Willcox, I heard stories of Geronimo and Cochise, and in Douglas, I listened to tales of Pancho Villa. I discovered historic restaurants in Jerome, a resurrected ghost town clinging to the side of a mountain, in cavernous train depots in Tucson and Prescott, and in grand old hotels in Bisbee and Douglas. I found other restaurants in pine-studded Flagstaff, among the red rocks of Sedona, and in the sprawling metropolis of Phoenix. More cafes and restaurants appeared in saloons and at old stagecoach stops, in adobe haciendas, mining camps, elegant Victorian homes, modest stone cottages, and glittering world-renowned resorts.

Some of these restaurants inhabit modest structures, reflecting the contribution of ordinary citizens to their town's development. At the El Charro Cafe, which is located in a small home in Tucson built over a century ago, the family tradition of hoisting fifty pounds of beef onto the roof each morning to dry in the sun—a crucial ingredient for the restaurant's famous Carne Seca—continues into its seventh decade. At the Carriage House, a quaint, century-old brick barn in Phoenix, the architecture reflects Arizona's booming capital city as it was at the turn of the twentieth century. And at Monti's La Casa Vieja, an old adobe hacienda, one can dine inside the former residence of Charles Hayden, the founder of Tempe.

During the preparation of this book, I was often asked, "What is it that makes a structure historic?" Obviously, age was a primary factor. The restaurants included in this book are all housed in buildings at least a half-century old. Many are much older, with some dating back to the 1800s. Other considerations were the building's architectural character and unique features. Many of these structures appear on the National Register of Historic Places and have been recognized as historically significant by various national, state, and local historic preservation organizations.

Another key factor used to determine a building's historic worth was the particular role a structure may have played in the town's development. Two restaurants which come to mind are at the Copper Queen Hotel in Bisbee and the Gadsden Hotel in Douglas, structures which served as the center of the towns' activities and as gathering places for traveling dignitaries and celebrities during the towns' heyday. Other structures that deserve historic consideration are some of the luxurious world-class resorts and guest ranches that sprouted onto Arizona's landscape in the 1920s and 1930s. These vacation spots established the state's reputation as an elegant winter paradise for wealthy snowbirds and celebrities seeking relief from cold winter temperatures.

Another requirement for inclusion in this book was the restaurant's willingness to share its recipes. With a few exceptions, the busy owners and chefs I approached were generous with both their time and talents, and they provided me with recipes that later won raves from family and friends when prepared in my own kitchen. I shall be forever indebted to those chefs who allowed me, notepad in hand, to follow them through their bustling kitchens and herb gardens, room-sized refrigerators and narrow corridors, as they shared cooking tips and enthusiasm for Arizona's native foods.

Arizona's native cuisine is solidly rooted in old Indian, Spanish, and Mexican traditions. The first staples were corn, beans, and chilies, a trio that still enjoys star billing in southwestern fare. Other standard items in most Arizona kitchens include tortillas, garlic, onions, cheese, tomatillos, avocados, cumin, and cilantro; and often, a long, red rope of chilies, called a *ristra*, is hanging near the doorway. Tortillas, the traditional staff of life in Arizona, often replace bread or rolls in southwestern kitchens. One of my fondest childhood memories is that of my classmate's mother preparing a stack of fresh tortillas in her Tucson kitchen for our after-school treat.

The earthy, robust flavors of southwestern cuisine have inspired many award-winning chefs to create their own distinctive dishes. At

Janos, a Mobil Four-Star restaurant in downtown Tucson, noted chef Janos Wilder combines classic French dishes with those of the Southwest. The cuisine at House of Trick's in Tempe blends southwestern flavors with those native to the Mediterranean region.

It is my hope that this book will serve as a travel guide to Arizona's fascinating historic restaurants and as a cooking companion in your kitchen. Because this book is subjective, not every historic restaurant in the state appears in this book. Some restaurants were not interested in participating or sharing their recipes. Others, although worthy candidates, were in transition and unable to participate.

Whether you dine at one of Arizona's historic restaurants, or enjoy a meal at home prepared from one of the recipes in this book, be assured that wonderful feasts await you. *Bien Comida*!

Acknowledgments

Special thanks go to:

Arizona's Office of Tourism for providing necessary information and assistance.

The various chamber of commerce offices, historic societies, and visitors' bureaus for providing important material on their particular city.

The restaurateurs for their enthusiasm for this project and for generously sharing their establishment's rich heritage.

The chefs for cheerfully contributing their recipes and secrets.

My supportive family and cherished friends, the willing guinea pigs who dined on the testing dishes and bolstered my confidence by asking for second helpings.

My editor, Andrew Waters, for his patience and guidance.

Dedication

To Dawn O'Brien,
whose affinity for historical settings
launched the series of books
on historic restaurants
and inspired the writing of this one.

Contents

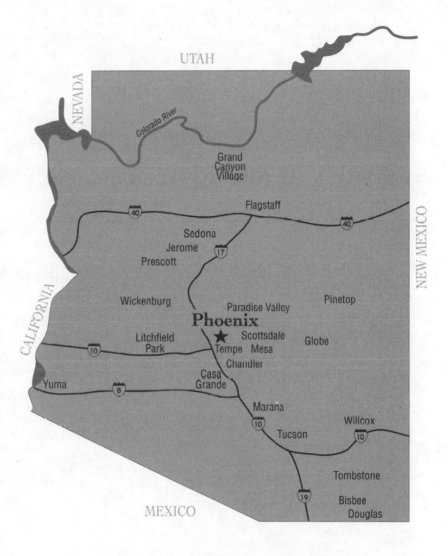

UTAH

NEVADA

Colorado River

Grand
Canyon
Village

Flagstaff

40

40

NEW MEXICO

Sedona

Jerome

17

Prescott

CALIFORNIA

Wickenburg

Paradise Valley

Pinetop

Phoenix

★ Scottsdale

Litchfield
Park

10

Tempe Mesa

Globe

Chandler

Casa
Grande

Yuma

8

Marana

10

Willcox

10

Tucson

Tombstone

19

Bisbee
Douglas

MEXICO

Arizona

Bright Angel Lodge Dining Room

Bright Angel Lodge
GRAND CANYON VILLAGE

It was stage-line owner J.W. Thurber who, in 1896, had the bright idea to provide lodging for passengers who rode his stagecoaches from Flagstaff to the Grand Canyon. He chose the name Bright Angel Hotel for his lodge at the canyon's south rim, although accommodations were hardly of the "hotel" caliber. Conditions were more of the camplike variety, consisting of a single cabin, which served as an office, and an assortment of tents. The misnomer was corrected a few years later in 1905, when the Fred Harvey Company assumed management of the Grand Canyon facilities and promptly renamed the primitive quarters with the more appropriate title of Bright Angel Camp.

Breakfast
6:30 A.M. until 11:00 A.M.

Lunch
11:15 A.M. until 4:45 P.M.

Dinner
5:00 P.M. until 10:00 P.M.

For reservations
(recommended
for lunch and dinner,
especially during summer months)
call (520) 638-2631

Considered unsightly by 1935, the original camp was replaced with the present log-and-native-stone structure and given its current name, Bright Angel Lodge. It was designed by architect Mary Jane Colter, a talented woman, whose work emphasizes nature's beauty over human's buildings. Although she is responsible for a number of the area's historic landmarks, Bright Angel Lodge is considered Colter's ultimate Grand Canyon achievement.

The pioneer-style lodge features a rustic lobby with log walls and furniture, a soaring ceiling, flagstone floors, and an enormous stone fireplace. Above the mantel hangs a striking wooden thunderbird, a mythical figure in American Indian mythology said to cause thunder and lightning. This winged creature, a familiar sight throughout the Southwest, also appears on a panel near the entrance to the Bright Angel Dining Room, located at the end of the hallway leading from the lobby.

Expecting to see a continuation of the lobby's rugged, "old lodge" atmosphere, I was surprised to find that the dining room sported a contemporary southwestern decor. A recent remodeling project, completed in the early 1990s, is responsible for the old restaurant's new look. The soft, muted tones of the desert appear throughout the spacious room. Log beams and pillars painted a pale-sand beige blend with windowed walls to provide an abundance of light. The result is an airy, casual atmosphere, highlighted by stunning views of the canyon.

A window seat at a comfortable booth overlooking a walkway and the canyon's rim is a perfect spot for viewing the canyon and its endless parade of visitors. It's also a great place to enjoy the restaurant's appetizing American and southwestern dishes. You'll find many old favorites on the menu, Barbecued Pork Spareribs, Braised Beef Tips and Rice, Rainbow Trout, club sandwiches, burgers, and a hearty Packer's Stew served in a bread loaf bowl. There's something for everyone, including a section entitled "Southwestern Selections" listing a half dozen or so Mexican dishes—Fajitas, Chimichangas, Tamales, Rellenos, and Enchiladas, most served with the standard rice and beans.

After hearing raves about the restaurant's Navajo Indian–inspired Fry Bread Taco, I was pleased to learn that the dish was the featured special on the day of my visit. The platter-sized mound of spicy, marinated chunks of chicken, chilies, beans, cheese, and salsa piled on top of a pizza-sized piece of puffy fried bread looked big enough to feed a tribe. Because the "Taco" was every bit as tasty as it looked, I had no problem finishing the whole plateful. My penalty for the overindulgence was that I had no room left for the restaurant's popular Apple Grunt Dessert, a scrumptious combination of apples, cinnamon, sugar, and oats baked in a cup and served warm with vanilla ice cream. To make sure there's plenty of room for this delicious treat on my next visit, I plan to reverse the order of my meal and order dessert first.

Bright Angel Lodge Dining Room's Fry Bread Tacos

1 cup milk
3 tablespoons molasses
2 tablespoons sugar
2½ teaspoons salt
½ cup warm water
1 ounce yeast

1 cup shortening
2¼ cups whole wheat flour
2¼ cups all-purpose flour
2 jalapeno peppers,
   chopped and seeded

*assorted grilled vegetables
   and/or meats, diced
cooked sausage
sliced tomatoes*

*chopped cilantro, or other herbs
refried beans
shredded cheese*

In 5-quart bowl, combine milk, molasses, sugar, salt, water, and yeast. Stir well and set aside. Allow mixture to stand for 30 minutes to allow yeast to bloom. Add ¼ cup shortening and mix at low speed. Add flours and jalapenos and mix for 5 minutes on medium speed. Turn dough out onto board, cover, and let rest 1 hour. Divide into 3 equal parts and roll with rolling pin into large pizza-sized rounds, sized to fit large skillet. Heat remaining shortening in skillet. Fry rounds until browned on both sides. Top with all or some of the toppings listed above, or be creative and add your own. Makes 3 large bread rounds.

Bright Angel Lodge Dining Room's Smoked Corn Relish

*4 ears of corn on the cob
½ cup red onion, diced small
¼ cup red bell pepper, diced
   small
¼ cup green bell pepper,
   diced small*

*¹/₃ bunch fresh cilantro,
   finely chopped
1 tablespoon rice wine vinegar
3 tablespoons olive oil
1 teaspoon Tabasco
salt to taste*

Grill corn in husks over smoke chips on grill or in smoker until done, about 20 to 25 minutes. Set aside. When cool, remove husks and silk fibers. Cut corn kernels from cobs. In a bowl, combine corn, onion, peppers, and cilantro. Add vinegar and oil, mixing well. Season with salt to taste. Use as a sauce on grilled seafood or chicken, or as a garnish in a light summer salad. Serves 8.

El Tovar Dining Room

El Tovar Hotel
GRAND CANYON VILLAGE

$\mathcal{V}$ery few restaurants can claim a view as awe-inspiring as the one at the El Tovar Dining Room. Sitting majestically on the rim of the Grand Canyon, this restaurant, located in the famous El Tovar Hotel, overlooks one of the world's geological marvels and most breathtaking sights, a mile-deep canyon where more than a billion years of time are exposed in colorful layers of rock.

The El Tovar was built in 1905, a few years after the Santa Fe Railroad arrived at the Grand Canyon. Constructed of native

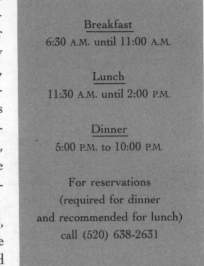

Breakfast
6:30 A.M. until 11:00 A.M.

Lunch
11:30 A.M. until 2:00 P.M.

Dinner
5:00 P.M. to 10:00 P.M.

For reservations
(required for dinner
and recommended for lunch)
call (520) 638-2631

stone and Oregon pine, the sprawling, multi-level hotel resembles a rustic European hunting lodge. Named after the Spanish explorer Pedro de Tovar, this historic landmark, known as the "architectural crown jewel of the Grand Canyon," has offered a host of amenities to its guests from the start. Along with spectacular canyon views, the hotel's earliest guests enjoyed electric lights powered by a steam generator, solariums, music rooms, and fresh water hauled by railroad from a point 120 miles away. Greenhouses and a dairy on the premises provided fresh fruit, vegetables, and milk products; and the "Harvey Girls," polished young ladies in prim black dresses with white collars and aprons, provided refined hospitality and gracious service. Operated under the management of the Fred Harvey Company from the start, the El Tovar has reigned as one of the grand old hotels of the West for over ninety years.

The El Tovar Dining Room is located at the rear of the hotel's handsome lobby, a rustic room featuring towering log columns, a massive stone fireplace, and stunning cowboy sculpture. A more refined rusticity graces the interior of the restaurant, which is a contrast of rough log walls and ceiling beams and tables formally dressed with fine linens, sparkling crystal, and elegant china.

To please the diverse palates of the canyon's visitors from all over the world, the restaurant offers exquisite continental dishes accented with flavors of the Southwest. The native influence is responsible for many of the restaurant's most popular dishes, like the cilantro-laced Black Bean and Crabmeat Cakes appetizers which are served warm and paired with an excellent Avocado Salsa. Entrées also sing with southwestern zing. My choice for an award goes to the tender Roast Duckling teamed with a Prickly Pear Jalapeno Honey. The chef, whose culinary wizardry is responsible for the restaurant's excellent meals, proudly boasts of using ingredients flown in daily to insure freshness and quality.

The interplay of sunlight and shadows on the walls of the Grand Canyon results in an ever-changing panorama. This historic restaurant, which would not exist without this scenic wonder, does its best to make the view available to its diners by serving meals from early morning to late evening.

El Tovar Dining Room's Southwestern Eggs

1½ pounds sausage
2 tablespoons mixed
  fresh herbs (chives,
  parsley, and thyme)
3 garlic cloves, minced
2 medium tomatoes,
  seeded and diced
½ medium red onion,
  diced
¼ cup plus 1 tablespoon
  fresh cilantro, chopped
juice from 2 limes

3 tablespoons olive oil
1 jalapeno, seeded and diced
salt and freshly
  ground pepper
4 tablespoons sour cream
2 tablespoons heavy cream
1 quart water
4 tablespoons white vinegar
4 eggs
2 yellow corn tortillas
2 blue corn tortillas
cilantro sprigs for garnish

Mix sausage, fresh herbs, and garlic together in bowl. Form into 4 patties and set aside. Prepare salsa in medium bowl by combining tomatoes, red onion, ¼ cup cilantro, lime juice, 1 tablespoon olive oil, jalapeno, salt, and pepper. Refrigerate until needed. In small bowl, stir together sour cream, heavy cream, and 1 tablespoon chopped cilantro. Season with salt and refrigerate until needed. Preheat oven to 400 degrees. In ovenproof pan, cook sausage patties in 2 tablespoons olive oil. Sear patties on both sides and bake in oven for 10 minutes. Drain on paper towels. In 1½- to

2-quart pan, bring water to a boil. Add vinegar and reduce heat to bring water to a simmer. Carefully break eggs into a small bowl and discard shells. Slide eggs into water and allow to simmer for 5 minutes. While eggs are simmering, heat tortillas slightly on warm grill or pan. With slotted spoon, remove eggs to a plate lined with paper towels. Place one yellow and one blue tortilla on serving plate side by side (overlapping if necessary to fit onto plate). Arrange 2 sausage patties in center of each plate. Top patties with 2 poached eggs and cilantro cream. Surround with salsa and garnish with cilantro sprigs. Serve immediately. Makes 2 generous servings.

El Tovar Dining Room's
Black Bean and Crabmeat Cakes with Avocado Salsa

1 pound black beans
4 cups water
1 medium onion, chopped
2 tablespoons garlic, minced
2 cups chicken stock
1 bunch fresh cilantro

1 cup lump crabmeat
2 tablespoons tabasco
1 tablespoon salt
flour
cooking oil or butter
Avocado Salsa (see recipe below)

Soak beans overnight in 4 cups water. Drain beans and discard soaking water. Cook beans, onions, and garlic in chicken stock over low heat until tender, about 1½ hours. Drain and cool. Run through a grinder on large die with cilantro. Add crabmeat and seasonings. Form into 16 equal patties. Dust with flour. Sauté a few minutes on each side until heated throughout. Top with avocado salsa. Makes 16 cakes or 8 servings.

Avocado Salsa

2 avocados, diced
½ medium red onion, diced small
1 medium red pepper, diced small
1 medium yellow pepper, diced small

½ bunch green onions, chopped
⅓ bunch fresh cilantro, chopped
1 tablespoon fresh lemon juice
¼ cup olive oil
2 tablespoons rice wine vinegar

Mix all ingredients together. Allow to sit for one hour before serving.

Charly's Restaurant and Pub

Weatherford Hotel • 23 North Leroux Street
FLAGSTAFF

The historic structure that houses Charly's Restaurant and Pub might not be standing today if it hadn't been for the city ordinance of 1897. The mandate, issued after a series of disastrous fires blazed through Flagstaff, required all new buildings in the business area to be built of brick, stone, or iron. The following year, merchant John Weatherford began construction on his two-story Victorian building, using brick.

Originally, the first floor was used as a general store, while the Weatherford family occupied the upper level. In 1899, a third story, to be used as a hotel, was added. The grand opening of the hotel was held New Year's Day, 1900. For many years, the Weatherford Hotel reigned as Flagstaff's finest hotel, serving as a social center for civic-minded locals and as a favorite stopover for traveling celebrities. A few of the famous who walked the halls of the Weatherford included Theodore Roosevelt, William Randolph Hearst, Wyatt Earp, and novelist Zane Grey, who reportedly wrote *The Call of The Canyon* in an upstairs bedroom.

In 1929, a fire destroyed the hotel's original cupola and three-sided balcony, a result, perhaps, of the notorious shootouts reported to have taken place there. By the 1930s, the glittering era of the Weatherford Hotel had ended, and the exterior was further altered. A layer of stucco was applied to the original sandstone facade, and in the 1950s, aluminum trim was added. Through the years, the structure has housed a theater, billiard hall, radio station, and a series of restaurants.

Today, Charly's Restaurant and Pub occupies the main floor of the old Weatherford building and traces of the hotel's glorious past re-

Winter Months

Lunch
11:00 A.M. until 2:00 P.M.
Monday through Friday

Dinner
5:00 P.M. until 10:00 P.M.
Monday through Friday

Saturday
11:00 A.M. until 10:00 P.M.

Summer Months

11:00 A.M. until 10:00 P.M.
Monday through Saturday

For reservations
(recommended)
call (520) 779-1919

main at the restaurant. The area just inside the entrance offers the best view of the handsome staircase, second floor landing, and original tin ceiling. Exposed brick walls, dating to the building's construction, appear throughout the two dining rooms and pub area.

The restaurant's downtown location and expanse of street-side windows make it an ideal spot for people watching, a pastime that escalates in warm weather when umbrellas appear on the front sidewalk and the area becomes an outdoor cafe. But it was cold the December day I arrived, and I was happy to see a roaring fire in the fireplace.

A hefty mug of Hot Buttered Rum was just what I needed to shake the chill from my bones. Now I understand why this creamy warmer-upper is such a popular item with the ski crowd, who annually flock to this town at the base of Arizona's highest mountains during snow season. The chef recommended the Brocco-Cheese Chicken and, in my book, produced a definite winner. The tender rolls of chicken, stuffed with three cheeses and broccoli and served over wild rice, were outstanding. The Carrot Cake being devoured at the next table looked so good, I ordered a slice too. Presto, another winner appeared, worth every calorie.

Charly's Restaurant and Pub's Hot Buttered Rum

1 cup (2 sticks) butter, softened
2 cups brown sugar
½ teaspoon vanilla
1 teaspoon cinnamon
pinch nutmeg
pinch ground cloves
pinch ground ginger
1 quart vanilla ice cream
8 ounces rum
hot water

Whip butter and sugar together until creamy. Add vanilla, cinnamon, nutmeg, cloves, and ginger and mix well. Add softened ice cream and continue to whip until well blended and creamy. Store in freezer container and freeze until firm. To serve, scoop portion of frozen ice cream mixture and drop into large mug. Fill with 8 ounces of hot water and 1 ounce rum. Stir and serve. Serves 8 to 10.

4 large eggs
1½ cups vegetable oil
2 cups baker's flour
2 cups granulated sugar
2 teaspoons double-acting
   baking powder
1½ teaspoons baking soda
1½ teaspoons salt

2 teaspoons ground
   cinnamon
2 cups grated carrots
1 cup crushed pineapple
1 cup grated coconut
½ cup walnuts, chopped
½ cup raisins

Preheat oven to 375 degrees. Combine oil and eggs in one bowl. Combine other ingredients in separate bowl. Mix ingredients in each bowl. Add oil-egg mixture to dry ingredients, blending slowly, a little at a time. Pour batter equally into two greased and floured 9-inch pans. Bake at 350 degrees for 45 minutes to 1 hour. Cool and spread with cream cheese frosting. Serves 10 to 12.

Cream Cheese Frosting

1½ cups cream cheese, softened
½ teaspoon vanilla
1½ cups vegetable shortening
½ teaspoon lemon juice

1 teaspoon lemon zest
½ cup butter, softened
4 to 5 cups powdered sugar

In large bowl, combine cream cheese, vanilla, shortening, lemon juice, lemon zest, and butter. Mix on medium speed until smooth. Slowly add powdered sugar until icing stiffens. Divide and spread over cool carrot cakes.

Chez Marc Bistro

503 North Humphreys Street (corner of Elm Street)
FLAGSTAFF

There's nothing quite like a jaunty French bistro for revitalizing tired palates. Flagstaff is fortunate indeed to have such a gem perched on a corner near the heart of downtown, in an old stone cottage.

John Milton Clark, a former United States deputy marshal, could hardly have been thinking of bistros when he built his seven-room craftsman bungalow and retaining wall of malpais rock in 1911. His sturdy structure, the first of its kind in the city, served as a home to a succession of owners until the mid-1980s. At that time, it was restored, converted into a restaurant, and awarded a listing on the National Register of Historic Places. The festive French touch appeared in 1991, when award-winning chef Marc Balocco purchased the cottage and cleverly transformed it into one of the classiest places in town.

Colorful umbrella tables scattered about the front patio and porch set the proper relaxed mood for the restaurant's charming country-French interior. Inside, two levels of dining in rooms with old wooden floors, stone fireplaces, and lace curtains provide a comfortable, home-like setting for the chef's imaginative dishes.

The chef, born and bred in France, has presided in some of the world's swankiest kitchens. His classic French cuisine is unmatched in a town that still has a frontier feel. For me, French bistros inspire thoughts of crepes and wine. I searched for both on the menu and found them. I could have chosen Crepes Bourguignonne with chunks of beef in a Burgundy wine sauce, or the Crepes du Pecheur, which featured a seafood medley in a delicate lobster sauce. However, I followed the chef's suggestion and ordered his special crepes du jour. The delicate blankets wrapped around tender chunks of chicken, tomatoes, and mushrooms and served with a flavorful herb sauce were superb. A glass of chilled Sauvignon Blanc, selected from the bistro's outstanding wine collection, proved the perfect accompaniment. Be-

Lunch
11:30 A.M. until 3:00 P.M.
Monday through Saturday

Dinner
5:30 P.M. until 9:00 P.M.
Monday through Thursday

5:30 P.M. until 10:30 P.M.
Friday and Saturday

For reservations
(recommended)
call (520) 774-1343

fore I had even finished my meal, I was planning a return trip. Next time I'll order the savory Stuffed Duck Legs with Polenta, a dish recommended by the chef, a man who certainly knows his way around a kitchen.

Chez Marc Bistro's Stuffed Duck Legs with Polenta

2 ducks (4½ pounds each)
¼ pound pork fatback
2 duck (or 4 chicken) livers
6 tablespoons crème fraîche
   or heavy cream
1 generous teaspoon fresh
   parsley, finely chopped
1 generous teaspoon fresh
   chervil, finely chopped
1 generous teaspoon chives,
   finely chopped
½ teaspoon thyme leaves
1 tablespoon cognac
pinch allspice
salt and pepper to taste
3 to 4 tablespoons cooking oil

3 medium tomatoes, chopped
1 small carrot, finely chopped
1 small onion, finely chopped
1 stalk celery, finely chopped
2 cloves garlic, crushed
bouquet garni
1 teaspoon tomato paste
7½ cups water
15 peppercorns
1 tablespoon butter
10 shallots, finely chopped
1 heaping teaspoon
   peppercorns, coarsely crushed
2 cups red wine
2 teaspoons thyme leaves

On a cutting board, remove the legs (with thigh portions attached) from the ducks. Set aside wings, neck, and carcass of one duck for stock. With a small, sharp knife, slit legs lengthwise on inner side. Carefully debone thigh, then drumstick without cutting drumstick apart or puncturing skin. Trim away fat and discard. Cut away half of meat from each leg, horizontally, as evenly as possible, and place in grinder or food processor. Add fatback and livers, and grind or process into a paste. Transfer mixture to a bowl and add cream, herbs, cognac, and allspice. Add salt and pepper and beat with a spoon for several minutes. Using kitchen string, tie small ends of each drumstick together. Spread legs out, skin side down, and lightly salt and pepper. Spread quarter of the stuffing out over each leg, then fold legs in half lengthwise so edges touch. With trussing needle and kitchen string, sew edges together to enclose stuffing, making 4 triangular pouches. Set aside.

Prepare stock by chopping reserved duck carcass, wings, and neck into pieces with cleaver. Place in large saucepan and brown in 1 to 2 tablespoons hot oil over low heat for 10 to 15 minutes. Add chopped tomatoes and boil for 8 minutes, stirring frequently to evaporate liquid. Add carrot, onion, celery, garlic, and bouquet garni. Simmer for 8 minutes to soften vegetables. Add tomato paste, water, a dash of salt, and 15 peppercorns. Raise heat and bring to boil, then reduce heat and boil slowly, uncovered, for 90 minutes. Skim off any foam that surfaces. Strain stock (there should be 2 cups) and spoon off any fat.

Heat 2 tablespoons of oil in ovenproof pot large enough to hold four legs in one layer with a little space around them. Season legs with salt and pepper, and prick each leg once with trussing needle. Place in hot oil and brown evenly over moderate heat for 8 minutes, turning legs over with wooden spoon. Remove and drain on paper towels. Pour off fat from pan and place pan over medium heat. Add 1 tablespoon butter, shallots, and teaspoon of peppercorns and simmer for about 5 minutes, or until shallots are soft. Add wine and raise heat. Boil rapidly for about 15 minutes, reducing until 1 tablespoon liquid remains. Preheat oven to 425 degrees. Place duck legs in pot with reduced wine mixture. Add stock, half covering legs. Add thyme leaves, cover pot, and bake for 30 to 35 minutes, or until done. Remove legs from pan and place on cutting board. Strain cooking liquid from pan into measuring cup and skim off fat. If necessary, boil liquid rapidly to reduce to 1 cup. Carefully remove strings from each leg. Spoon a small portion of the sauce onto each dinner plate. Place stuffed duck leg on each plate and serve with homemade polenta. Serves 4.

Chez Marc Bistro's Polenta

6 cups water
½ teaspoon salt

2 cups coarse-grained cornmeal
2 to 3 tablespoons butter

Bring water to a boil in heavy pot. Add salt and turn heat down until water is simmering. Add cornmeal in very thin stream, stirring constantly with long wooden spoon. Continue stirring for about 15 minutes, until polenta tears away from sides of pot. Pour polenta onto cookie sheet and spread evenly, about ¾-inch thick. Allow to cool. Cut into desired shapes with cookie cutter. Melt butter in skillet or sauté pan. Add polenta pieces and sauté until lightly browned on each side, adding more butter if necessary. Serves 4.

Cottage Place Restaurant

126 West Cottage Avenue
FLAGSTAFF

lagstaff has been a stopover for sightseers en route to and from the Grand Canyon since the late 1800s, when stage-coaches began bouncing passengers over rugged trails to the canyon's south rim. Today, visitors travel to the canyon in air-conditioned comfort over smooth highways, but many still consider Flagstaff, with its endless supply of motels and restaurants, a convenient stopover point.

Dinner
5:00 P.M. until 9:30 P.M.
Tuesday through Sunday

Closed
Monday and major holidays

For reservations
(recommended)
call (520) 774-8431

You won't find the historic Cottage Place Restaurant, one of the town's best-kept secrets, on the main thoroughfare. Instead, look for it across the tracks, tucked away on a quiet neighborhood street not far from the Northern Arizona University campus. This award-winning restaurant, housed in a handsomely preserved structure that dates back to 1908, is a favorite with locals and visitors seeking a gourmet dining experience in an unhurried atmosphere.

The brown-and-white cottage, framed by a low stone wall, was the first house to appear on this modest residential side street. The warmth and charm of a family home still remain throughout the inviting rooms, which have been converted into a romantic restaurant by Executive Chef Kurt Gottschalk and his wife, Sharley.

Because the rooms are small, with only a few tables, dining becomes an intimate affair. Locals report that the best tables are on the front porch, where you can watch the sunset and observe the sidewalk activity. However, it really doesn't matter where you sit, because every nook and cranny of this cozy restaurant is inviting. Flowered wallpaper and lace curtains provide an attractive backdrop for tables draped in pink and white linens. Add the flickering candles and fresh flowers and you have the perfect setting for the restaurant's exquisite cuisine.

The chef, a native of Holland, apprenticed and worked in some of the finest kitchens in Holland and the United States. His traditional and innovative dishes continue to thrill the palates of his faithful Flagstaff following—who seem quite happy to keep the restaurant a secret from the crowds.

Crudités and a tasty pâté arrive along with a menu that features a tempting array—mainly consisting of continental dishes. You'll find a few wonderful sounding items from the chef's homeland, and a few dishes featuring the flavors of the Southwest. Although all meals include homemade soup, a tossed green salad, a fresh garden vegetable, and a choice of potato du jour or rice pilaf, this is a place for pleasantly whiling away the hours, so an appetizer is in order. Anyway, it's hard to resist Baby Artichokes marinated with tomatoes, mushrooms, and spices, or the Smoked Rainbow Trout with Pickled Beets, or Escargots in Garlic-Herb Butter with Sour Dough Slices.

The chef's mastery in the kitchen is most apparent in the excellent entrées, which feature meat and poultry in delicately seasoned wine sauces. Veal Regina, a delightful combination of scallops of veal loin, sautéed with tomatoes, mushrooms, pistachio nuts, and herbs and served with a delicious wine sauce, had my taste buds singing with the first bite. I knew, long before I finished my meal, that I wanted to return soon to try another one of the chef's creations, perhaps the Schnitzel or maybe the Scampi.

Cottage Place Restaurant's Dutch Herring Salad

22 ounces pickled
   herring filets, diced small
2 large tart green apples,
   diced
1 medium red onion, diced
1 tablespoon lemon juice

1 tablespoon sugar
2 cups sour cream
1 teaspoon white pepper
1 teaspoon parsley flakes
lettuce leaves

Garnish

tomato slices
hardboiled egg slices

olives
pickles

Combine herring filets, apples, onion, lemon juice, sugar, sour cream, pepper, and parsley flakes in bowl and mix well. Divide into serving portions and serve on a bed of garnished lettuce. Serves 6 to 8.

4 tablespoons flour
½ teaspoon salt
½ teaspoon white pepper
8 veal loin medallions,
*   3 ounces each*
1 tablespoon butter
1 teaspoon oil
½ red onion, sliced
4 large mushrooms, sliced

6 sun-dried tomatoes,
*   julienned (¼ cup)*
¹/₈ cup pistachio nuts
¹/₂ cup dry marsala wine
1 cup veal stock
1 tablespoon pesto sauce
½ teaspoon salt
sprigs of fresh basil
*   for garnish*

Prepare coating for veal by combining flour, salt, and ¼ teaspoon white pepper. Coat veal pieces in flour mixture. Heat butter and oil in sauté pan. Add veal and sauté on both sides until golden brown. Remove veal from pan and set aside. Add onion, mushrooms, tomatoes, and nuts to pan and deglaze with wine. Add stock, pesto, salt, and remaining ¼ teaspoon white pepper. Simmer for 5 minutes. Add the sautéed veal and simmer additional 5 minutes. Divide veal medallions among 4 plates and spoon sauce over top. Garnish with sprigs of basil. Serves 4.

Historic Saginaw House Restaurant

717 West Riordan Road
FLAGSTAFF

The vast ponderosa pine forest at the northern edge of Flagstaff was responsible for the area's first permanent settlement, as well as the state's first large-scale industrial enterprise — a sawmill. It was during the prosperous days of the early 1900s, when timber was king, that the structure known today as the Historic Saginaw House Restaurant was built. Originally, it was situated in the neighborhood of Milltown, which was then a separate community from Flagstaff.

Dinner
5:00 P.M. until 10:00 P.M.
Daily

For reservations
(recommended)
call (520) 774-3929
or (520) 774-4804

The bright-blue, multi-leveled home, trimmed in creamy white, still seems to possess an air of stately reserve that sets it apart from the hustle and bustle of this busy university town. Surely, back in the 1930s when a workday at the mill was twelve hours long and the typical wage was fifteen cents per hour, this spacious residence must have been considered a grand mansion. Today, it remains a tribute of sorts to the home's earliest residents and reminds the diner of the founding families who helped establish Milltown-Flagstaff as an economic force.

This regal residence was built in 1914 by the Arizona Lumber and Timber Company for J.B. Koch, the manager of the lumbermill located up the street. From his broad, raised front porch, Mr. Koch easily could have kept an ear tuned to mill operations and a watchful eye on the world's largest stand of milled ponderosa pines located a stone's throw away. The J.B. Dolan family moved into the house in 1933 after Mr. Dolan bought 51 percent of the mill. Less than a decade later, the mill was leased to the Saginaw-Manistee Lumber Company. Eventually the lumbermill was closed and moved to another location.

One of the structure's original three levels was lost when a fire raged through the residence in 1927. Thanks to recent remodeling efforts by the current owner, the former cellar has been transformed into a colorful saloon, bringing the number of levels in the building back to three.

The air outside was cool and crisp on the day I visited the Historic Saginaw House Restaurant, but inside the mood was friendly and cozy. Pleased with my window-side seat in a lovely room named after Mrs. Dolan, I sipped my cup of steaming hot coffee and paused to admire the refined, turn-of-the-century atmosphere. This room, like the other dining rooms located on the first floor and the bed-and-breakfast inn on the second floor, features original wood floors, working fireplaces, and interesting antique furnishings. It was a perfect setting to enjoy one of the Historic Saginaw House's memorable meals.

For my entrée, I chose the Chicken Hunter Style, the undisputed favorite of the local crowd. After the first, savory mouthful of brandy-flamed chicken sautéed in a garlic and butter sauce with tomatoes and mushrooms, I understood why. I also knew that I had to have the recipe. Next time, I'll try another house favorite, the White Zinfandel Scampi served over angel hair pasta. To sustain me until the next visit, the chef generously agreed to provide the recipe.

Historic Saginaw House Restaurant's White Zinfandel Scampi

½ cup butter (1 stick)
¼ cup flour
3 to 4 chopped scallions,
    white part only
½ cup white zinfandel wine
1 tablespoon brandy

2 cups whipping cream
1 pound medium shrimp,
    peeled, deveined, and cooked
1 pound bay scallops, cooked
1 pound angel hair pasta,
    cooked al dente

Prepare roux in small sauté pan by melting ¼ cup (½ stick) butter over very low heat. Add flour and whisk gently, blending until mixture is smooth. Remove from heat, set aside, and keep warm. In medium saucepan, melt remaining butter over low heat. Add chopped scallions and simmer for 2 minutes. Stir white zinfandel wine and brandy into mixture, remove from heat, and allow to cool. In separate saucepan, warm whipping cream gently over low heat. Slowly whisk in cool brandy/wine mixture and allow to cook until mixture begins to bubble around edges. Whisk roux into mixture, a tablespoon at a time, and simmer for 3 minutes until thickened. Add shrimp and scallops and simmer until thoroughly warmed, about 1 to 2 minutes. Serve over warm angel hair pasta. Serves 4 generously.

Historic Saginaw House Restaurant's Chicken Hunter Style

1 cup butter (2 sticks)
¼ cup flour
4 chicken breasts,
   boneless and skinless
1 tablespoon garlic,
   finely chopped
1½ cups whole mushrooms

1 cup tomatoes, chopped
2 cups commercial
   au jus or beef broth
1 cup whipping cream
black pepper to taste
1 to 2 teaspoons
   kitchen bouquet

Make a roux by melting ¼ cup butter in small saucepan and adding ¼ cup flour. Whisk until well blended. Set aside and keep warm. Melt remaining butter over medium heat in large sauté pan or skillet. Add chicken breasts and cook over low heat until brown on both sides, about 5 minutes on each side. Remove chicken, set aside, and keep warm. Add garlic to skillet and cook over low heat for 2 to 3 minutes until golden. Add mushrooms and tomatoes. Cover and simmer until soft, about 2 to 3 minutes. Stir in au jus and allow mixture to simmer for 10 minutes. Warm whipping cream gently over low heat in small saucepan. Slowly whisk whipping cream into au jus mixture. Stir in kitchen bouquet. Blend roux, a little at a time, into mixture with whisk, stirring until smooth. Simmer gently for approximately 6 to 8 minutes, allowing mixture to thicken. Add browned chicken breasts and simmer in sauce for approximately 2 minutes. Divide into 4 servings and serve sauce over chicken breasts. Serves 4.

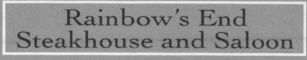

Rainbow's End
Steakhouse and Saloon

3235 West Highway 89A
SEDONA

11:00 A.M. until 10:00 P.M.
Daily

For reservations
call (520) 282-1593

$\mathcal{S}$edona's famous red-rock cliffs and sandstone formations, which change colors according to the season and time of day, provide a magical setting for this picturesque town. On the winter afternoon I arrived at the Rainbow's End Steakhouse and Saloon, the rocks were a deep, rosy pink, creating a colorful backdrop for dining or, perhaps, filming a western movie.

John Wayne, Henry Fonda, and Glenn Ford were just a few of the big-name cowboy stars who bellied up to the bar at the Rainbow's End. Also a favorite with locals, this entertaining place has been a gathering spot and social center for area residents since a saloon, dance hall, and skating rink were added to the original structures in the 1940s.

Originally built in the early 1900s as a homestead for a family named Gibson, the expansive structure of today was then only two small, separate buildings—a residence and a general store. The old homestead once served as a stagecoach stop and, after World War I began, a military registration point. It was finally converted into a restaurant in the 1940s. Through the years, the two structures were expanded and united. In 1990, the new owners began another extensive remodeling project, adding a new kitchen and remodeling the dance hall which had been unused for over twenty years. The result is a sprawling complex that includes a restaurant, saloon, dance hall, and outdoor dining patio.

If you arrive on horseback, just tie up your mount at the wooden rail in front of the restaurant. Otherwise, park your buggies in the lot and mosey on in for one of the biggest, juiciest steaks around. The large room that makes up the main restaurant is somewhat more polished than the saloon or dance hall, but it's every bit as western. Scattered about the rough, wood-panelled room are old saddles, an antique stove, framed photos, and lots of cowboy gear.

This place is proud to be western and rustles up the kind of grub that would make anyone want to make their home on the range. Expect to be enticed by the irresistible sights, aromas, and sounds of sizzling steaks and lip-smacking ribs being served at surrounding tables. I was unable to resist such tempting fare and ordered the special of the day, the Chile-stuffed New York Steak. Believe me, cowboy grub doesn't get much better than this thick, tender, perfectly grilled steak oozing jack cheese and spiked with green chile. My dining companion sang similar praises over her Smoked Baby Back Ribs, another house favorite. Fish and fowl fans have not been forgotten, and the menu also lists some interesting garden salad entrées and a handful of items for children, who are considered "little pards" at Rainbow's End. Dinners are accompanied by crisp garden salads or soup, cowboy beans, and corn on the cob; and the wine list offers an interesting variety of beer, wines, and specialty drinks.

Before saddling up and riding off, consider your sweet tooth and ask about the Rainbow's End's fabulous cobbler desserts. A bowlful of steaming cherries under a pastry crust topped with a melting mound of vanilla ice cream can add the perfect ending to a memorable meal. On weekend evenings, shuffle on back to the dance hall, the area's largest, where the foot-stompin' country-western music provides an opportunity to work off the calories. Don't be concerned if you don't know how to do the two-step, just fake it like others out on the floor.

Rainbow's End Steakhouse and Saloon's Chile-stuffed New York Steak

*1 New York strip steak
(12 to 14 ounces)
1 whole green chile (canned)*

*1 strip jack cheese
(3½ inches by 1 inch)*

Create a pocket in the steak by slicing lengthwise on one side of steak to within a ½ inch of each end. Drain chile and slice open. Stuff chile with cheese rectangle. Tuck cheese-filled chile into steak pocket. Grill on barbecue until cheese is melted and meat has reached desired degree of doneness. Serve hot. Serves 1 generously.

Rainbow's End Steakhouse and Saloon's Raspberry Cobbler Pastry

Pastry

1¼ cups self-rising flour
½ teaspoon salt
⅓ cup shortening
¼ cup sugar

2 tablespoons vanilla extract
1 tablespoon almond extract
4 tablespoons water

In medium bowl, combine flour, adding a little at a time, with salt, shortening, sugar, vanilla and almond extracts, and water. Mix, preferably with dough hook, until dough is firm but still moist and tacky. Set bowl in refrigerator to chill slightly while preparing filling.

Filling

3½ cups frozen raspberries
¾ cup sugar
1½ cups water

2 tablespoons cornstarch
3 tablespoons butter

In saucepan, combine raspberries, sugar, and 1¼ cups water. Bring to boil over medium heat. In small bowl, blend cornstarch with remaining ¼ cup water until smooth. Add to raspberry mixture and stir until thickened. Pour filling into a 9- by 6½-inch baking dish. Roll out dough to ¼-inch thickness and lay over filling. Melt butter, brush over top of dough, and sprinkle with additional sugar. Bake in 350-degree oven for 1 hour or until golden brown. Serves 8 to 10.

The Jerome Grille

309 Main Street
JEROME

$\mathscr{N}$o book about historic buildings in Arizona would be complete without mentioning the old mining town of Jerome. This unusual, picturesque city, once known as America's largest ghost town, literally clings to the side of a mountain. The city is so rich in history that the entire old town has been designated a National Historic Landmark.

8:00 A.M. until 8:00 P.M.
Daily

For reservations (unnecessary)
and information
call (520) 634-5094
or (800) 634-5094

When mining operations began around Jerome in 1883, it was discovered the town was perched above a vast deposit of copper. In the years that followed, billions of dollars' worth of copper were produced from over eighty-eight miles of underground tunnels. The mines boomed and blasted for over seventy years. They attracted so many saloons, gambling halls, and bordellos that Jerome was referred to as "the wickedest town in the West." Raging fires devastated the clapboard town three times before 1900. Earth-shaking dynamite blasts during the days of open-pit mining caused a portion of the business district to slide downward into new locations across the road. By the time the mines finally closed in 1953, the population had plummeted from a 1920s peak of fifteen thousand to a mere fifty, and Jerome's status fell from boom town to ghost town. But Jerome's survival instinct was strong, and the forgotten town eventually became a haven for the counterculture pioneers of the 1960s and 1970s. Abandoned homes were renovated, old shops were reopened, and the town was brought back to life as a thriving community of artists and writers. Eventually, Jerome became noted for its colorful shops, galleries, small inns, and casual restaurants.

The historic J. H. Clinkscale Building, which today houses The Jerome Grille, is another example of the town's resilience. Erected over the ashes of a devastating fire in 1899, the structure was made of poured, reinforced concrete with walls up to eighteen inches thick to make it as fireproof as possible. The building was named after its builder, an insurance adjuster named J. H. Clinkscale, and originally housed a hardware store on the lower level and offices upstairs. Through the years, various businesses occupied the structure, including a mortuary and a hotel. Today the old Clinkscale Building, recently painted a pleasant shade of pale green, houses an inviting restaurant on the ground floor and a charming, eight-room inn on the second.

A refreshing simplicity rules the decor throughout the restaurant's two rooms—a lounge and a main dining room that are divided by a wall. Original wood floors still creak underfoot, and an interesting collection of photographs from Jerome's mining heyday lines the thick old walls. I could have easily slid into one of the comfortable booths. However, I opted for a table by the front window where I could watch the endless parade of tourists winding their way along the sloping streets. Across the street, a vacant lot marks the spot where a row of businesses once stood before dynamite blasts caused them to slide down the slope. One can only imagine the shock and terror of occupants on this side of the street as they watched the familiar buildings slip out of sight.

The Jerome Grille is noted for serving wonderful southwestern dishes, which I might add, can also be colorful. A case in point is the appetizer, Espinaca con Queso, a creamy sauce flavored with jalapeno cheese and spinach that arrived in a crisp tortilla shell surrounded by red, green, and white tortilla chips—the colors of the Mexican flag. I turned to my dining companion, Don Hopkins, one of the restaurant's owners, for an entrée suggestion. He recommended the Clinkscale Chicken, a flavorful dish featuring grilled chicken stuffed with herb-flavored goat cheese and topped with a lively romesco sauce. If you appreciate the robust flavor of goat cheese, this dish is a must; and paired with perfectly steamed broccoli, spaghetti squash, and a baked potato, the meal proved worthy enough to carry the original name of this historic building.

Feeling full, I had no intention of sampling another morsel. Then the Deep-Fried Ice Cream arrived, a favorite of Don's sweet-toothed wife, Carla. This festive looking confection, a crisp tortilla bowl cradling a ball of ice cream coated in a crunchy, cinnamon-and-honey-laced crust and topped with whipped cream and a cherry, looked almost too perfect to touch. But because I considered it my duty to make sure everything tasted as good as it looked, I decided on a spoon-sized sample. You may rest assured that this delicious dessert's flavor did, in fact, match its appearance, all the way down to the last cinnamon-flavored crumb.

The Jerome Grille's
Espinaca Con Queso (Spinach with Cheese)

¼ cup butter
½ cup onions, chopped
1 tablespoon green onions,
   finely chopped
¼ cup fresh garlic, minced
2 tablespoons fresh
   cilantro, chopped

½ teaspoon ground cumin
1 pound fresh spinach
1½ cups heavy
   whipping cream
1¼ pounds Monterey
   Jack cheese with jalapenos
tortilla chips

Melt butter in saucepan over low heat. Add onions, garlic, cilantro, and cumin. Sauté until vegetables are soft. Clean spinach, remove stems, and chop. Add spinach to butter mixture, stirring until wilted. Add cream and simmer 25 minutes, stirring occasionally. Add cheese and stir until cheese is melted. Serve with tortilla chips for dipping.

The Jerome Grille's Deep-Fried Ice Cream

½ pound corn flakes cereal
1½ quarts French vanilla
   soft-serve ice cream
4 cups vegetable oil
6 pre-formed tortilla bowls
   (optional, available in
   specialty stores)

²/₃ cup honey
1 tablespoon ground cinnamon
6 tablespoons sugar
1 cup whipped cream
6 sweet, fresh cherries
   for garnish

Crush cornflakes with rolling pin or mash flakes into small pieces in large bowl. Use ice cream scoop and hands to form ice cream into 6 round balls. Roll ice cream balls in crushed flakes, covering completely. Freeze overnight until hard. In 2-quart pan, heat oil to boiling. Drop frozen ice cream balls, one at a time, into oil for 3 seconds only. Remove with slotted spoon or tongs. Place each ball in a tortilla bowl or ice cream sundae dish. Pour an equal amount of honey over each ice cream ball. Mix cinnamon and sugar together and sprinkle over each serving. Top each serving with dollop of whipped cream and a cherry. Serves 6.

P. Faires

Dining Car Cafe

100 East Sheldon Street
PRESCOTT

*L*adies and gentlemen may now share a table in the same room at the Dining Car Cafe. But that hasn't always been the case at this imposing Prescott landmark, the former depot for the Santa Fe, Prescott, and Phoenix Railroad. Back in 1907, when this "modern" concrete terminal was constructed to replace the former wooden depot, women were not allowed to smoke. Since men faced no such restriction, a separate lobby was built for ladies. This private chamber provided ladies with an exclusive waiting area away from the distasteful fumes of the male smokers, and solved the dilemma of how to accommodate both sexes at the same depot. Reportedly, the "Ladies Lobby" also provided a refuge for women wishing to escape any unpleasantness caused by rowdy menfolk who may have overimbibed at the saloons on nearby Whiskey Row.

Lunch
11:00 A.M. until 4:00 P.M.
Thursday through Monday
May through October

Dinner
5:00 P.M. until 8:30 P.M.
Thursday through Monday
May through October

For reservations
call (520) 778-5488

The impressive southwestern-style structure featuring a red-tile roof was obviously built to last. The building's walls and floors are composed of solid concrete, both inside and out. The spacious two-story depot has a total of fifteen rooms and three vaults. The vault on the lower level, where the walls measure more than two feet in thickness, serves as the restaurant's business office. The lobbies now house the restaurant, which expands outdoors during pleasant weather onto the former boarding area of the depot. The railroad tracks that once ran beside this dining patio were removed in 1991, but if a certain group of preservation-minded citizens have their way, the tracks will return and the trains will run again.

True to its name, the Dining Car Cafe offers its diners an imaginary trip aboard a luxury train of yesteryear. Transforming the lobbies of this former depot into the intimate atmosphere of a railroad dining car was no easy feat, but it has been cleverly achieved by the talented owner. Rich shades of burgundy and hunter green appear in the window curtains and table linens, and on display throughout the two dining rooms are interesting items from the owner's collection of railroad memorabilia. The old ticket booth, cash register, and the authentic railroad china provide a glimpse into Prescott's past. This attention to detail should have you properly prepared for dinner aboard a train.

In the evenings, when miniature lights twinkle and soft strains of classical music drift through the rooms, the restaurant takes on a special glow that borders on romantic. A blackboard at the entrance announces the evening's menu, a limited but tempting selection of meat, seafood, fowl, and pasta dishes. Following the chef's recommendation, I ordered Lamb Chops with Rosemary-Port Sauce. The rejoicing began with the first whiff of herb-and-wine-flavored sauce and continued until the last bite of tender lamb had disappeared. Let others sing the praises of the restaurant's celebrated Beef Wellington and Southwestern Chile-Stuffed Chicken Breast; I'll order this delicious lamb dish again on my return visit.

Breakfast is also a crowd-pleaser at the old depot, especially for those with hearty appetites and a sweet tooth. These early birds are known to satisfy their sugar cravings with heaping platefuls of the cafe's Almond Joy and Chocolate Chip Pancakes topped with nuts, whipped cream, and shredded coconut. The lunch crowd also dines in style, choosing from a menu listing sandwiches named after railroad items, crepes, and frittatas.

Dining Car Cafe's
Lamb Chops with Rosemary-Port Sauce

1 cup port wine
1 sprig fresh rosemary
1 teaspoon dried rosemary
1 tablespoon cornstarch

¼ cup cold water
8 loin lamb chops
rosemary sprigs for garnish

In small saucepan, combine port with a rosemary sprig and dried rosemary. Reduce by half over low to medium heat. Dissolve cornstarch in cold water. Stir into port and bring to boil. Cook for 1 minute. Broil or grill lamb chops to preferred stage of doneness. Spoon sauce over chops. Garnish with fresh rosemary sprigs. Serves 4.

Dining Car Cafe's
Southwestern Chile-Stuffed Chicken Breast

1 large yellow bell pepper,
   roasted, peeled, and seeded
1 large red bell pepper,
   roasted, peeled, and seeded
3 Anaheim chilies
3 tablespoons canola oil
1 small jalapeno, cored,
   seeded, and minced
2 cloves garlic, minced
½ small red onion,
   chopped fine

½ teaspoon chili powder
salt and pepper to taste
2 tablespoons cilantro
½ cup pine nuts, toasted
4 boneless, skinless
   chicken breasts
   (6 to 8 ounces each)
²/₃ cup sour cream

Divide yellow and red peppers, setting aside half of each for later use. Dice remaining peppers and Anaheim chilies. In medium sauté pan, add canola oil, and sauté jalapeno, garlic, and onion for 4 to 5 minutes. Add diced bell peppers, chilies, chili powder, salt and pepper, cilantro, and pine nuts and stir. Remove from heat and set aside. Pound chicken breasts until fairly thin. Cover half of breast with stuffing and fold over other half. Bake at 375 degrees for 20 to 25 minutes. In blender or food processor container, blend remaining red bell pepper with ¹/₃ cup of sour cream until smooth. Remove from container and set aside. Rinse container and repeat process with yellow pepper and remaining ¹/₃ cup of sour cream. Slice each chicken breast crosswise into ¹/₂-inch medallions. Arrange on plate and pour yellow and red pepper sauces in criss-cross pattern over top. Serves 4.

Gurley St. Grill

230 West Gurley Street
PRESCOTT

he Gurley St. Grill, a stunning, bright-pink building with snappy green-and-white awnings, evolved from the ashes of a devastating fire that swept through Prescott in 1900. The blaze destroyed many downtown structures, including the Mulvenon Saloon, a wood-frame building at the corner of Gurley and Granite Streets. A sturdier, two-story brick building was constructed in its place. When this building opened a year later, a new watering hole, the Gurley Street Bar, occupied the ground floor. Upstairs, a brothel offered furnished rooms for rent by the week, day, or hour. Undoubtedly, the structure's upper-level activities and its location a block away from the rowdy saloons on "Whiskey Row" contributed to its decline into skid-row status, where it was to remain for a number of years.

Lunch
10:45 A.M. until 4:00 P.M.
Daily

Dinner
4:00 P.M. until 10:00 P.M.
Daily

Late Night Menu
10:00 P.M. until Midnight

For reservations
call (520) 445-3388

Today, it's hard to imagine the impressive structure in skid-row condition. In 1991, ninety years after its birth, the neglected but architecturally-sound building caught the eye of Paul Murphy. This Arizona native with a passion for Prescott's history recognized a historic gem in need of polishing, as well as an opportunity to contribute to the rehabilitation of the downtown area. Inspired by his success with another thriving restaurant in a historic Prescott building—a restored mercantile building located a few blocks away—Murphy launched a restoration project to convert the run-down building into an award-winning restaurant.

The transformation of the old saloon into an exciting restaurant featuring original brick walls, beamed ceilings, and an exposed kitchen area was no simple task. However, the painstaking efforts undertaken to maintain the structure's architectural integrity did not go unnoticed. In 1993, Gurley St. Grill received the Governor's Award for Historic Preservation, and it is also listed on the National Register of Historic Places.

The restaurant's happy-go-lucky, pub atmosphere vibrates with laughter and lively conversation. It's a place to meet friends, sample a brew from the wide selection of micro-brewed beers, and feast on the restaurant's popular assortment of casual and light dishes. The menu offers an interesting array of appetizers, pasta dishes, sandwiches, individual pizzas, specialty burgers, and grilled seafood and meats. Beer is the big item here, especially if brewed at one of Arizona's own micro-breweries. "Gurley St. Gold" and "Prescott Red" seem to be the favorite brews with the local crowd. If beer doesn't excite you, perhaps the refreshing Passion Fruit Iced Tea will. Either drink makes a tasty accompaniment for the restaurant's signature dishes. It was a toss up as to which dish was best, the spicy Sonoran Black Bean Chili, served alone or over a mound of fresh pasta and renamed Chili Mac, or the creamy Sonoran Corn Chowder. The warm, savory garlic bread sticks also win raves and requests for seconds. If you happen to resist your server's recommendation to try one of the scrumptious homemade desserts, you'll have another chance to surrender on your way out. A pastry display with a wondrous assortment of fresh-baked goodies waits near the exit and has been known to topple the resolve of even the most steadfast dieters.

Gurley St. Grill's Creamy Corn Chowder

1 tablespoon olive oil
1/2 cup onion
1 cup green chilies, diced
1 15-ounce can whole
    kernel corn (with liquid)
2 1/2 cups water
2/3 cup half-and-half
1/4 teaspoon liquid smoke
1/4 teaspoon white pepper

1/2 teaspoon fresh
    parsley, chopped
1 tablespoon chicken base,
    or bouillon granules
2 tablespoons cornstarch
1 cup mild cheddar
    cheese, grated
2 1/4 cups cooked
    potatoes, diced

Heat olive oil in soup pot. Add onion and chilies and sauté until onion is transparent, about 1 to 2 minutes. Add corn and corn liquid and stir. Add 2¼ cups water, half-and-half, liquid smoke, pepper, parsley, and chicken base or bouillon. Bring to low boil. Dissolve cornstarch in remaining ¼ cup cold water and add to soup mixture. Stir and cook until slightly thickened. Add grated cheese and potatoes. Stir until mixture is well blended and potatoes are heated through. Makes about 2½ quarts.

Gurley St. Grill's Banana Walnut Bread Pudding

4 eggs
1½ cups white sugar
1 tablespoon vanilla
2 teaspoons nutmeg
2 teaspoons cinnamon
1 tablespoon melted butter
2½ cups milk
½ cup walnuts, chopped
1 cup banana slices

8 cups bread cubes
  (French or sourdough
  work best)
1 cup softened butter
1 cup powdered sugar
3 tablespoons Captain
  Morgan's Spiced Rum
  (may substitute Amaretto
  or Frangelico liqueur)

In large bowl, mix eggs, white sugar, vanilla, nutmeg, cinnamon, melted butter, milk, walnuts, and banana slices together until blended. Add bread cubes and mix until bread starts to break up. Do not overmix. Pour into pre-greased 8- by 12-inch baking dish. Bake at 350 degrees for 1 to 1¼ hours. Make sauce by whipping softened butter and powdered sugar in bowl until fluffy. Slowly mix in rum or liqueur. Divide pudding into portions and top with butter-rum sauce. Serves 4 to 6 generously.

Murphy's

201 North Cortez Street
PRESCOTT

ack in 1890, when J.I. Gardner opened his store in downtown Prescott, he hardly could have known that his motto, "All goods guaranteed to be first class," would still be intact a century later. However, his now legendary words did survive, along with his distinctive brick-and-masonry store. Today, his store is regarded as one of the Southwest's best and oldest examples of an existing mercantile building.

Gardner designed his structure around a cast-iron storefront, ordered from a St. Louis catalog and delivered by rail. The building's strategic location between the train station and the courthouse was a guarantee for success at the store, which offered everything from hardware and crockery to groceries and dry goods. When Gardner finally retired in 1918, the structure was sold and became a secondhand store.

In 1984, a preservation-minded entrepreneur named Paul Murphy began the challenge of restoring the grandeur of the old building. The result of his painstaking attention to detail is a structure that appears much as it did a hundred years ago. The cast-iron storefront remains, along with the original entrance doors, pressed-tin ceiling, and Gardner's old office. You'll also find the same floor-to-ceiling shelving and the skylit mezzanine at the building, now listed on the National Register of Historic Places.

The building currently houses Murphy's self-named, award-winning restaurant. The atmosphere of Murphy's is an exciting mixture of nineteenth-century charm and contemporary brass and sass, a combination that makes this restaurant a particular favorite with tourists. Some come to visit the spacious, gleaming bar where they can choose from over sixty brands of imported, domestic, and micro-

Lunch
11:00 A.M. until 3:00 P.M.
Daily

Dinner
4:30 P.M. until 10:00 P.M.
Sunday through Thursday

4:30 P.M. until 11:00 P.M.
Friday and Saturday

4:30 P.M. until 11:00 P.M.
Every day during
summer months

Sunday Brunch
11:00 A.M. until 3:00 P.M.

For reservations
(recommended)
call (520) 445-4044

brewed beer including Murphy's special house brew. Others come for the restaurant's highly acclaimed prime rib and seafood dishes and for the congenial atmosphere. My husband, Jon, and I came for all of the above.

As ceiling fans rotated overhead, we studied the menu from a high-backed wooden booth. The restaurant features a wide selection of popular American-style dishes. The appetizer list includes a variety of interesting selections ranging from Bay Shrimp Nachos to Escargots, but when Murphy's signature dish, Tortilla Soup, was mentioned, my choice was made. Deciding on an entrée selection was a tougher call because everything on the menu looked appealing— pasta dishes, seafood, mesquite-broiled steaks, smoked baby-back ribs, and stir-fried combinations. After some deliberation, I settled on the Seafood Brochette with skewered shrimp, scallops, fish, and vegetables, while my hungry spouse ordered a thick, juicy, perfectly prepared steak. We had no trouble polishing off the main course or the crisp garden salads and the loaf of warm bread that was included with our entrées.

After our memorable meal, a toast seemed in order. So, raising our glasses of Arizona-brewed Murphy's Mile High Lager, we saluted this first-class restaurant's decision to honor the same motto that was established within the walls of this old building more than a century ago.

Murphy's Tortilla Soup

2 tablespoons olive oil
½ bell pepper, diced
½ cup celery, chopped
½ cup yellow onion, diced
1½ cups tomato purée
¹/₄ cup green onion, chopped
¹/₃ cup Ortega green chilies, chopped
³/₄ cup tomato juice
1 quart water
1 teaspoon chicken base, or bouillon granules

1 teaspoon beef base, or bouillon granules
½ teaspoon oregano
¼ teaspoon garlic salt
¼ teaspoon black pepper
½ teaspoon coriander
1¼ cups tomatoes, diced
¾ cup whole kernel corn
crisp tortilla chips and shredded Monterey Jack cheese for garnish

Heat olive oil in large saucepan over medium heat. Add bell pepper, celery, and yellow onion and sauté for 1 to 2 minutes until onions are transparent. Add tomato purée and sauté 5 minutes. Add green onion, chilies, tomato juice, water, chicken and beef base or bouillon, oregano, garlic salt, pepper, coriander, diced tomatoes, and corn. Allow soup to come to a boil. Remove from heat. Place handful of tortilla chips in each serving bowl. Pour soup over chips and sprinkle with shredded cheese. Makes approximately 2 quarts.

Murphy's Salmon Burgers

1 pound fresh salmon
  meat, poached
¾ cup cracker meal
1 egg, lightly beaten
2 tablespoons red onion,
  finely diced
2 tablespoons celery,
  finely diced
2 tablespoons mayonnaise
1 tablespoon
  Worcestershire sauce
1 tablespoon yellow
  prepared mustard

1 teaspoon cayenne
  pepper sauce (mild type,
  Red Devil is good)
1 teaspoon salt
¼ teaspoon black pepper
4 slices havarti or
  muenster cheese
4 lemon slices
4 hamburger buns,
  kaiser rolls,
  or favorite bread

In bowl, use fork to break poached salmon into small pieces. Mix in remaining ingredients, blending until mixed well enough to form into patties. If mixture is too dry, add additional mayonnaise, a little at a time. If too wet, gradually add more cracker meal until desired consistency is reached. Divide mixture into 4 equal portions and press down to form patties about ½-inch thick. Grill patties on broiler or in skillet with 1 to 2 teaspoons of oil. Heat over medium-high until lightly browned. Top with a slice of havarti or muenster cheese and serve with a lemon slice. Serve alone or on your favorite bread or roll. Makes 4 burgers.

P. Faires

Peacock Room at
The Hassayampa Inn

122 East Gurley Street
PRESCOTT

The roots of the city of Prescott lie in the nearby Hassayampa River, where a party of prospectors discovered gold in 1863. The following year, the town became Arizona's first territorial capital, and the stage was set for Prescott's ensuing days as a notorious boom town.

By 1927, the civic-minded residents of Prescott were anxious to dispel the rough-and-rowdy reputation of the town's territorial days. The horseless carriage and the state's expanding highway system provided the means for Phoenix-area families trapped in the scorching desert heat to escape to pleasant, mile-high Prescott. It was a perfect time to impress the sophisticated Phoenicians and capitalize on the town's location at the same time. The ambitious community made the daring decision to erect a splendid, four-story hotel in the heart of town, one they hoped would be considered the grandest in Arizona. The community hired one of the most distinguished architects of the day, a Texan by the name of Henry Trost, to design the hotel. However, they promptly altered his original Spanish-revival design by selecting an exterior of ruffled brick in order to reflect the town's midwestern origins. When it was finished, the Hassayampa Inn with its cupolated bell tower, copper cornices, porte-cochere, and hand-painted lobby ceiling was, indeed, an impressive structure. The hotel attracted tourists and celebrities, as well as local citizenry who used the splendid inn for the town's social center.

Like many of Arizona's historic buildings, the Hassayampa Inn suffered during the 1960s and 1970s as it passed through a succession of owners. A costly restoration in 1986 bankrupted the owner,

Breakfast
7:00 A.M. until 11:00 A.M.
Monday through Friday

7:00 A.M. until 11:30 A.M.
Saturday and Sunday

Lunch
11:00 A.M. until 2:00 P.M.
Monday through Friday

Noon until 2:00 P.M.
Saturday and Sunday

Dinner
5:00 P.M. until 9:00 P.M.
Sunday through Thursday

5:00 P.M. until 9:30 P.M.
Friday and Saturday

For reservations
(recommended)
call (520) 778-9434

and the inn was eventually purchased by Bill and Georgia Teich, an astute and preservation-minded couple. In their competent hands, the grande dame of Prescott is thriving once again.

To reach the Peacock Room, the inn's historic restaurant, from the handsome lobby, follow the hallway once known as "peacock alley" (a name which comes from the blue-green tiles appearing in the hallway steps). Although the once infamous Whiskey Row is only a block or so away, here in this lovely, high-ceilinged room, with its brass chandeliers and plush, rounded booths, refinement reigns. Servers in black and white and tables adorned with pink linens and rose-tinted stemware add to the air of distinction that places this restaurant in a class of its own.

From a menu listing an intriguing selection of continental selections, I chose the Red Mountain Trout, a dish that has earned the restaurant's executive chef, Linda Rose, an enthusiastic following. I added my name to her growing list of fans as soon as I took the first delicious bite of tender trout, which arrived steaming under a blanket of spinach and prosciutto. Along with my entrée came a loaf of hot-from-the-oven bread, a bowl of vegetarian split-pea soup, and a salad. The perfect accompaniment to this fantastic meal was a glass of chilled Chateau St. Jean 1991 Fume Blanc, just one of the many fine selections from the excellent wine list.

As I glanced around the room, I thought again about the status-conscious citizens responsible for this lovely Prescott landmark. They would be proud to know that their beloved inn's Peacock Room is still creating such an elegant impression.

Peacock Room at the Hassayampa Inn's Red Mountain Trout

2 fresh trout
  (about 10 ounces each)
2 tablespoons butter
½ red onion, diced
¼ pound prosciutto,
  chopped

pepper to taste
½ pound fresh spinach
3 to 4 tablespoons
  vegetable oil
½ cup all-purpose flour
¼ cup white wine

Clean and dress trout. Rinse in cold water and keep trout covered and cool. Melt butter in sauté pan and add onion. Sauté for

2 minutes. Add prosciutto, pepper, and spinach leaves. Sauté briefly, about 1 minute, making sure not to wilt spinach and allowing it to keep its color. In large skillet, heat vegetable oil over medium heat. Dredge trout in flour and cook in oil, flesh side down, for approximately 3 minutes. Flip trout. Add wine and cook for 3 minutes until cooked through. Remove from pan and place on serving plate. Surround or top trout with spinach, prosciutto, and onion mixture. Season with pepper before serving. Serves 2 generously.

Peacock Room at the Hassayampa Inn's Veal Piselli

½ cup all-purpose flour
salt and pepper to taste
½ pound veal medallions
   or scaloppine
3 tablespoons butter
   or butter substitute
¼ cup red onion, chopped

½ teaspoon garlic butter
¼ cup mushrooms, sliced
dash of sherry
$^1/_8$ cup veal stock
$^1/_2$ cup fresh or
   frozen green peas

Season flour with salt and pepper. Coat veal pieces with flour. Melt butter in sauté pan or skillet over medium-high heat. Add veal and sauté quickly on both sides. Add onion, garlic butter, mushrooms, and sherry. Turn heat to low and allow wine to reduce for 1 to 2 minutes. Add veal stock, peas, and salt and pepper. Cook until peas are heated through but still crisp, approximately 1 to 2 minutes. Serves 2.

Willow Creek Restaurant

2516 Willow Creek Road
PRESCOTT

When I first saw the Willow Creek Restaurant, a stately old home nestled into a hillside beside a creek, it seemed perfectly suited to its country setting. You can imagine my surprise at discovering the romantic, gable-roofed house once stood on a corner near the heart of downtown Prescott.

Although the structure dates back to 1877, the identity of the original owners is a mystery. A dreadful fire wiped out the entire business district and the city directory records in 1900, taking the identity of the first owners of the house with it. Once known as the "Reibling House," the structure reportedly served at various times as a hospital, nursing home, bordello, Sunday school, and apartment house.

10:30 A.M. until 9:00 P.M.
Monday through Saturday

9:00 A.M. until 9:00 P.M.
Sunday

For reservations
call (520) 778-7686

In 1962, the historic house was moved to its present hillside site in the community of Willow Creek north of Prescott and converted into a restaurant. During the 1970s, a century after its construction, the building underwent an extensive renovation project. The original walls and floors were reinforced, endless layers of paint were removed, and the woodwork was restored to its natural finish. Today, the impressive results are evident throughout the restaurant's inviting interior and storybook exterior. The narrow wooden bridge spanning the creek in front of the building adds another layer of charm to the setting.

The restaurant's interior reflects Prescott at the turn of the twentieth century, blending Victorian primness with rustic comfort. Delicate lace curtains, Tiffany lamps, flowered wallpaper, and old historical photographs are found throughout the two levels of dining. I was seated in the former downstairs parlor, which has been expanded and now serves as the restaurant's spacious dining lounge. From my table, I had a view of the original fireplace and the framed portrait of the "ghost of Willow Creek" that hangs above the mantel. The phantom reportedly guards over the restaurant's guests. Another old photograph worth noting is the one of "Little Egypt," the notorious belly dancer who is said to have caused quite a stir during her performance in 1910 at the Palace Bar on Prescott's infamous Whiskey Row.

Char-broiled steaks, cornfed and perfectly aged, are the pride of the restaurant's kitchen, and a heavy favorite with the local dinner crowd. Seafood fans praise the yummy Beer Batter Islandic Cod, a fish-and-chips idea borrowed from British pubs. I would have ordered the cod if a plateful of wonderful-smelling pasta hadn't passed by on the way to another table. I simply couldn't resist the wonderful aroma of the Italian Sausage Fettuccine laced with spinach, wine, cheese, and pesto. My enthusiasm for the dish did not go unnoticed. I was rewarded with the chef's recipe, which has now become a family favorite.

Willow Creek Restaurant's Italian Sausage Fettuccine

2 to 3 tablespoons olive oil
1 pound Italian sausage,
    cooked and drained
½ cup onion, chopped
½ cup green pepper, chopped
½ cup zucchini, chopped
½ cup mushrooms, sliced
2 tomatoes, cut into wedges
1 teaspoon Italian seasoning
1 tablespoon garlic,
    finely diced

2 tablespoons quality
    commercial pesto sauce
½ cup Chablis wine
½ cup cooked spinach
1 cup V-8 juice
12 ounces fettuccine,
    cooked al dente
¼ cup Parmesan cheese,
    grated

Heat olive oil in large sauté pan. Add sausage, onion, green pepper, zucchini, mushrooms, and tomatoes. Cook for approximately 3 minutes until vegetables are tender but still crisp. Add Italian seasoning, garlic, and pesto sauce. Mix well. Add wine, spinach, and V-8 juice. Cook, stirring occasionally, for 3 to 5 minutes until all ingredients are well blended. Combine with cooked fettuccine. Toss and mix well. Divide into 4 servings and top with Parmesan cheese. Serves 4.

Willow Creek Restaurant's Black Peppercorn Steak

3 tablespoons olive oil
2 heaping tablespoons
  crushed black peppercorns
4 rib-eye steaks
  (8 ounces each)
2 tablespoons fresh
  garlic, finely diced

¼ cup onion, finely diced
1 tablespoon flour
½ cup Chablis wine
1 cup au jus
2 tablespoons A-1 sauce
2 tablespoons butter

Heat olive oil in large sauté pan. Rub crushed peppercorns into steaks. Cook steaks in olive oil, browning on both sides, until cooked to desired degree of doneness. Remove steaks, set aside and keep warm. Stir garlic and onion into pan juices. Add flour, whisking and blending into a roux. Add wine, au jus, and A-1 sauce. Stir and cook over low heat until blended and heated through. Stir in butter and return steaks to pan to reheat. Serve sauce over steaks. Serves 4.

Willow Creek Restaurant's Garlic Chicken

2 boneless, skinless
  chicken breasts
  (6 to 8 ounces each)
1 tablespoon olive oil
2 tablespoons
  fresh garlic, finely diced
1 tablespoon onion,
  finely diced

2 tablespoons tomato pieces,
  finely diced
½ cup Chablis wine
1 pinch chicken base,
  or bouillon granules
2 tablespoons butter

Trim visible fat from chicken and pound to flatten. Set aside. Heat olive oil in sauté pan. Add chicken and cook a few minutes on each side to brown. Add garlic, onion, and tomato. Deglaze pan with Chablis. Add chicken base or bouillon and butter. Continue cooking a few minutes until flavors are blended. Put 1 chicken breast on each serving plate and top each serving with ½ portion of sauce. Serves 2.

P. Faires

Charlie Clark's Steak House

1701 East White Mountain Boulevard (Hwy. 260)
PINETOP

The history of Charlie Clark's Steak House, a sprawling log structure in the White Mountain town of Pinetop, is steeped in stories of moonshine and mischief. It begins in 1928, back in the days of prohibition, when two log cabins were combined to form a gathering place where illegal corn squeezings flowed from a barrel hidden beneath the bar. When prohibition was finally repealed, the former speakeasy went legitimate and became known as Jake Renfro's Famous Log Cabin Cafe.

Dinner
5:00 P.M. until 9:00 P.M.
Monday through Thursday

5:00 P.M. until 10:00 P.M.
Friday and Saturday

For reservations
(recommended)
call (520) 367-4900

In 1938, the business was sold to Charlie Clark, a cattleman and cook who turned the cafe into a steak house. Fast food was of no interest to old Charlie who prepared the steak dinners himself, peeling potatoes and putting together salads, one at a time, after orders were taken. While Charlie cooked, customers poured their own drinks at the same bar that once concealed moonshine. That same bar is still in use today. In 1952, Charlie was laid to rest a half mile up the road, but his reluctant spirit reportedly remained behind. For years after his death, the pesky ghost was blamed for mysterious happenings at the steak house—pictures toppled from walls and stove burners ignited for no apparent earthly reason.

Charlie's ghost doesn't come around much anymore, at least since the current owners, Bill and Tricia Gibson, assumed operation of the restaurant in 1981. Perhaps the spirit's disappearance is a result of the Gibsons' decision to preserve Charlie's name and to allow his favorite food, steaks, to dominate the menu.

The frontier ambience of the restaurant continues in the original rooms, which were remodeled in the 1970s to remove traces of a massive fire that swept through the building. Comfortable booths and tables are paired with interesting southwestern furnishings ranging from Indian kachina dolls and cowboy gear to a pot-bellied stove and mounted animal heads.

Mesquite-broiled steaks, grilled to order, have been the pride of the kitchen since 1938 and still pack in the crowds today. Sizzling top sirloin, rib eye, T-bone, New York strip, filet mignon, and prime rib are available in generous sizes and served "Western Style," with sautéed bell peppers, onions, sliced mushrooms, and salsa. My choice, a "ladies cut" of Roast Prime Ribs of Beef Au Jus served with creamy horseradish, was so tender that I didn't really need my steak knife.

Although the main focus here is on beef, the chef also wins raves for his excellent "Sea and Streams" dishes. I've already decided that the next time I dine at Charlie Clark's I'll have the King Salmon Steak, which can be ordered mesquite-broiled, baked, or poached and is served with hollandaise sauce. The Trout Barnie, a house specialty featuring sautéed trout with crab, asparagus, hollandaise sauce, and toasted almonds, ranks a close second on my list of things to sample.

Those who arrive with an appetite for fowl also have an excellent assortment of dishes from which to choose. From what I could determine, mesquite-broiled chicken seems to be the heavy favorite, but the Long Island Roast Duckling, served on wild rice with a choice of raspberry, orange, Montmorency, or banana sauce, also looked very tempting. Because Pinetop's cool mountain air is a favorite vacation spot for Phoenix residents looking to escape the desert's summertime heat, the restaurant is prepared to accommodate a variety of appetites, including vegetarians and those seeking special "health-conscious" dishes.

The restaurant's most recent addition, a spacious room added at the back of the structure in 1981, is another reason Charlie Clark's continues to draw crowds. Along with the drinking and dining, there's also some off-track betting—some call it gambling—going on in back, which somehow seems fitting at an establishment founded for mischief.

Charlie Clark's Steak House's Cajun Shrimp Diane

24 jumbo shrimp	4 bulbs fresh shallots, diced
¾ cup (1½ sticks) butter or margarine, melted	16 large fresh mushrooms, sliced
Cajun spice	1 pound linguine, cooked al dente
4 cloves fresh garlic, diced	

Peel and devein shrimp. Dip shrimp in melted butter or margarine. Then dip in Cajun spice to coat. Set aside. Pour remaining melted butter into large skillet over medium heat. Add shrimp, garlic, shallots, and mushrooms. Simmer until shrimp are cooked and turn pink, about 3 to 4 minutes. Additional melted butter may be added to pan if more "sauce" is desired. Toss pasta with shrimp and butter sauce. Divide pasta and shrimp mixture into 4 equal portions and serve. Serves 4.

Charlie Clark's Steak House Roast Pheasant Smitane

2 carrots, peeled
2 stalks celery
1 large onion, peeled
2 whole pheasants
    (2½ to 3 pounds each)
salt and pepper to taste

2 tablespoons fresh garlic,
    minced
8 slices smoked bacon
1 cup water
½ cup Sauterne wine

Slice carrots, celery, and onions into thin julienne strips and set aside. Preheat oven to 375 degrees. Rinse pheasants in cool water and place in small roasting pan. Salt and pepper cavity of each pheasant. Add julienne celery, carrots, onion, and minced garlic to cavity. Drape bacon strips over top of pheasants. Add water and Sauterne wine to roasting pan. Cover with foil and place in oven. Reduce oven temperature to 350 degrees and bake for approximately 1½ to 2 hours, or until tender. Remove foil wrap and allow pheasants to brown lightly. Remove from oven and split pheasants in half, allowing ½-pheasant per serving. Serve with Smitane Sauce. Serves 4.

Smitane Sauce

2 tablespoons butter
2 tablespoons onion,
    finely chopped

3 cups commercial brown sauce
1½ cups sour cream
½ cup Sauterne wine

Melt butter in large saucepan over low heat. Add onion and simmer until transparent. Add brown sauce, sour cream, and wine. Stir to blend and simmer until hot. Divide sauce into 4 equal portions and serve with pheasant.

The March Hare

170 West Wickenburg Way
WICKENBURG

If The March Hare had been around back in 1863, when frustrated prospector Henry Wickenburg was combing the desert for gold, he may have been too busy enjoying the fare at this quaint tearoom to discover the precious nugget that launched a gold rush and caused a town to be given his name. Legend has it that the determined miner finally found gold in a rock he had thrown at a bothersome vulture, an event which led to Arizona's richest gold-producing mine—appropriately named the Vulture Mine.

Brunch
9:00 A.M. until 11:00 A.M.
Tuesday through Saturday

Lunch
11:00 A.M. until 2:00 P.M.
Tuesday through Saturday

For reservations
(recommended)
call (520) 684-0223

The March Hare, a delightful tearoom in a small house built in 1925, wasn't around to lure Henry away from his desert digs, but it's attracting a strong following today. Built as a winter residence for a family named Echeverria, it is considered an excellent and unique local example of the brick-bungalow style. The home's distinctive architecture has earned it a spot on the National Register of Historic Places. The structure served as a residence until 1993, when it was converted into an appealing Victorian tearoom, a rare gem in a town that prides itself on its mining and dude-ranching heritage.

The tearoom is named after the floppy-eared rabbit that appears in *Alice in Wonderland,* and the restaurant does its best to recreate a storybook atmosphere. The romantic interior features three petite dining rooms and a tiny gift shop, all with the original wood floors. Lace covers the windows and tables, and plain walls have been cleverly enhanced by the addition of carved mantelpieces, stencils, and interesting wall decorations. My favorite room was painted a deep forest green and trimmed with a flowered border. Classical music adds a soothing touch, and scented candles from the gift shop at the rear provide the sweet and spicy scent that permeates the interior.

The word "tearoom" usually has me thinking of ladies sipping tea from china cups and nibbling on exquisite delicacies. The March Hare not only upholds this vision, but expands it by adding substantial brunch and luncheon meals, including old-fashioned favorites that are anything but dainty. Scalloped Ham and Potatoes and Chicken Noodle Soup was the featured special on the day I visited The March Hare. The menu also lists the standard luncheon fare—Quiche; a Chicken Salad with Apples and Nuts; a Ham, Cheese, and Avocado Sandwich; and a few salad selections. I noted from the menu's flip side that, had I arrived in time for brunch, I could have selected fresh-baked scones, sticky buns, breakfast breads, homemade granola, or Belgium waffles.

I finally decided on the Scalloped Ham and Potatoes, with a sample of the Chicken Salad with Apples and Nuts and a slice of Lemon-Glazed Zucchini Bread. Keeping with the tearoom tradition, my luncheon arrived looking as good as it tasted, and a glass of raspberry iced tea provided the perfect accompaniment. Don't plan to pass up dessert, especially if the Brownie Chocolate Chip Cheesecake is being offered. It's the perfect item for any tea party. Alice would have loved it in Wonderland, and so will your family and friends when you prepare the recipe that follows.

The March Hare's Brownie Chocolate Chip Cheesecake

1 small package
   fudge-brownie mix
3 packages (8 ounces each)
   cream cheese, softened
   at room temperature

1 can (14 ounces)
   sweetened condensed milk
3 eggs
2 teaspoons vanilla
½ cup mini chocolate chips

Preheat oven to 350 degrees. Grease bottom of 9-inch springform pan. Prepare brownie mix as package directs. Spread in pan and bake 35 minutes, or until set. Remove from oven and set aside. While brownie mix is baking, beat cream cheese in large mixing bowl until fluffy. Gradually add condensed milk, mixing well. Add eggs and vanilla, mixing until well blended. Stir in chips. Pour mixture over brownie shell. Reduce oven temperature to 300 degrees. Bake 50 to 60 minutes, or until center is set. Allow to cool, then chill thoroughly in refrigerator. Makes one 9-inch cheesecake.

The March Hare's Broccoli Salad

1 cup mayonnaise
½ cup sugar
¼ cup white vinegar
2 large heads (about 5 cups)
  fresh broccoli florets

1 red onion, thinly sliced
1 generous cup pecans,
  chopped
1 pound cooked bacon,
  crisp and crumbled

Prepare dressing (best made a day ahead and refrigerated) by mixing mayonnaise, sugar, and vinegar together in small bowl. In large bowl, combine broccoli, onion, pecans, and bacon. Pour dressing over broccoli mixture and toss well. Serves 6 to 8.

The March Hare's Lemon-Glazed Zucchini Bread

2 cups flour
1 cup sugar
1 teaspoon baking soda
¼ teaspoon salt
½ cup yogurt or sour cream
¼ cup melted butter

2 tablespoons grated
  lemon peel
1 cup zucchini, shredded
½ cup powdered sugar
juice of 1 lemon

Preheat oven to 350 degrees. Mix flour, sugar, baking soda, and salt together in bowl. Add yogurt or sour cream, butter, 1 tablespoon lemon peel, and shredded zucchini. Mix until well blended. Pour into greased 9-inch square pan or loaf pan. Bake 35 to 40 minutes for square pan, or 45 to 50 minutes in loaf pan. While bread is baking, mix powdered sugar, lemon juice, and remaining 1 tablespoon grated lemon peel to form glaze. While loaf is still warm, puncture with fork and frost with glaze. Makes 1 loaf.

Arcadia Farms Cafe

7014 East First Avenue
OLD TOWN SCOTTSDALE

*O*ld Town Scottsdale does its best to live up to its image as "the West's most Western town." A favorite with visitors, it's a shopper's paradise with block after block of porch-fronted stores displaying western wear, Indian crafts, and southwestern art. After awhile, too much of anything, even the Old West, can be tiring, and many shoppers yearn for an escape. Arcadia Farms Cafe provides the perfect antidote, a refreshing breath of country-French air.

The engaging, petite cafe is housed in a modest home that was constructed in the 1930s of slump block and brick. It served as a residence for a family named Burkett and later was operated as a preschool and an antique shop. The cafe's present owners, who purchased the small home and the two apartments located at the rear of the structure in 1988, had no intention of converting the various buildings into a restaurant. Instead, they envisioned a catering business that also offered takeout service. As planned, a catering service offering a takeout menu opened after completion of a two-year renovation project. Regular patrons had other ideas, however, and preferred to remain on the premises while they enjoyed their savory food. Eventually the catering business was moved to a new location across the street, and the Arcadia Farms Cafe was opened.

The irresistible smell of bread baking in the oven welcomed me into the inviting environs of the restaurant. Wonderful breads are the cafe's forte and the pride of the kitchen. They have earned this restaurant a strong following. Each day features different fresh-baked breads, and a blackboard, entitled "Our Daily Breads," reveals the current selection. The tastefully decorated country-French interior features old plank flooring, handsome antique furnishings, attractive straw-flower arrangements, and linen-covered tables. Light classical music adds a restful touch; its calming effect is felt throughout the three cozy rooms and the romantic outdoor patio.

Breakfast
8:00 A.M. until 3:00 P.M.
Monday through Saturday
Year-round

Dinner
6:00 P.M. until 9:00 P.M.
Monday through Saturday
November through May

For reservations
(recommended)
call (602) 941-5665

Since the cafe opened, its cuisine continues to score points with the local crowd and also earns rave reviews from visitors. Just reading the "Lunch at the Farm" menu is enough to set your taste buds roaring. There are so many marvelous choices to choose from—sandwiches made from herb-seasoned, homemade focaccia breads; savory soups; and divine salads featuring exciting combinations of vegetables, fruits, meats, and pasta. And hardly a chile pepper to be found.

The featured soup on the day I visited the cafe was a flavorful blend of tomatoes, wild rice, and fresh basil. The soup proved to be a tasty prelude to my luncheon entrée, a Grilled Salmon Salad. Consider yourself blessed if the delicious combination of crisp greens, dill-seasoned penne pasta, and chunks of marinated, grilled salmon is on the menu when you arrive. Like the cafe's breads, desserts are a must. If you've overindulged and left no room for one of these exquisite treats, plan to stop at the glass dessert case near the front door and select a take-home purchase from the tempting display of scones, tortes, tarts, cakes, and pies.

Arcadia Farms Cafe's Walnut Bread

*1 tablespoon dry yeast
   (or two ¼-ounce packages)
2 tablespoons sugar
¼ cup warm water
2 tablespoons butter*

*2 cups milk
2 cups bread flour
2 cups whole-wheat flour
2 teaspoons salt
1 cup walnuts, chopped*

Combine yeast, sugar, and warm water in a small bowl. Whisk well and proof (allow to stand) for 5 minutes. Melt butter in a medium to large pan. Add milk and warm, but do not boil. Combine flours and salt in large mixing bowl. Add milk-butter mixture and mix, preferably with dough hook. After a few turns, add proofed yeast. Knead until smooth and elastic. Add walnuts and continue kneading until completely incorporated and dough comes away from sides of the bowl. Turn into a greased bowl. Grease the bottom of the dough, then turn it over. Cover bowl with plastic wrap and let dough rise until doubled in bulk. Punch down, roll into a loaf, and place into greased loaf pan. Allow to rise again.

Halfway through second rising, cut diagonal slashes ½-inch deep and 1-inch apart in top of the loaf. When risen, bake for 35 minutes at 350 degrees. Cool on a rack. Makes 1 loaf.

Arcadia Farms Cafe's Scones

2¼ cups all purpose flour
1 teaspoon baking powder
¼ teaspoon baking soda
1 tablespoon sugar
pinch salt

½ cup (1 stick)
　unsalted butter
½ to ¾ cup heavy cream
1 small egg
2 tablespoons light cream

Sift dry ingredients into large mixing bowl. Cut butter into mixture. Add heavy cream and mix lightly with fingers until dough holds together. Wrap in plastic wrap and chill for 30 minutes. Roll dough into a circle about ½-inch thick for small scones, or ¾-inch thick for larger scones. Cut dough into desired shapes and place on sheet pan lined with parchment paper. Prepare glaze by mixing egg and light cream together in small bowl until well blended. Brush across tops of scones with pastry brush. Bake at 375 degrees for 13 to 15 minutes or until scones are golden brown. Makes about 20 scones.

Arcadia Farms Cafe's Apricot Bread

1½ cups dried apricots
2¼ cups all-purpose flour
1 tablespoon plus
　2 teaspoons baking powder
½ teaspoon salt
½ teaspoon baking soda

¾ cup sugar
1 cup buttermilk
1 egg, beaten
1 tablespoon butter, melted
½ cup pecans, chopped

Cook apricots according to directions on package. Cut apricots into thin strips and dredge in ½ cup flour. Sift remaining 1¾ cups flour, baking powder, salt, baking soda, and sugar together. In separate bowl, combine buttermilk and egg and mix well. Add to flour mixture. Add butter and mix. Fold in pecans and apricots. Pour mixture into greased 9- by 5-inch loaf pan. Bake for 1 hour at 350 degrees. Makes 1 loaf.

Los Olivos Mexican Patio

7328 East Second Street
OLD TOWN SCOTTSDALE

$\mathcal{L}$os Olivos Mexican Patio, a popular restaurant and night club in Old Town Scottsdale, is named after the century-old olive trees that once enclosed a forty-acre orange grove. A nasty drought in the late 1890s wiped out the orange grove, but the olive trees remained. These hearty symbols of Scottsdale's agricultural foundation can now be seen running down the center of Second Street, and they provide the setting for the story of Los Olivos Mexican Patio.

11:00 A.M. until 10:00 P.M.
Sunday through Thursday

11:00 A.M. until 11:00 P.M.
Friday and Saturday

For reservations
(recommended on weekends)
call (602) 946-2256

The story begins in 1919, when Tomas and Cecilia Corral moved their eight children from a small mining town in Sonora, Mexico, to the farming community of Scottsdale. The family pitched their tents under the olive trees and found work in the cotton fields of the area. A few years later, with their combined earnings, the industrious family managed to purchase two lots nearby. In 1928, they built a sun-baked adobe building on one of the lots, and the seeds for Los Olivos Mexican Patio were planted.

The Corral's homestead quickly became a social center for other Mexican families in the barrio. They came to mingle under the olive trees, dance on the dirt floors, and feast on traditional home-made tamales and enchiladas. Over the years, the structure served as a meeting place of various forms for the community. It was used as a pool hall and later served as a chapel, dance hall, labor meeting hall, and a bakery. In 1946, members of the Corral family opened Los Olivos as a beer and wine bar, and in 1953, a restaurant was added to the original structure. Today, third generation Corral-family members operate the restaurant, and their combined talents are evident throughout the sprawling facility.

Bold concrete sculptures and a wrought-iron canopy of colorful glass panels announce the restaurant's entrance. Inside the thick walls is a delightful Mexican cantina, where the decor is Mayan-inspired, the food Sonoran-Mexican, and the beat, especially on weekends, a lively Latino.

I dined in the structure's oldest room, now the restaurant's main dining room, where dark, exposed beams stretch across the ceiling and hand-painted Mexican mirrors and ropes of dried red chiles, called *ristras*, adorn the stucco walls. Desiring something authentic and different, I took my server's suggestion and ordered the Sonora Enchilada. This dish, prepared from an old Corral-family recipe, differed from a typical enchilada of rolled corn tortillas filled with cheese and meat. Instead it featured a flat, fried corn cake smothered in spicy red chile sauce and topped with cheese, onion, lettuce, and tomato. If you've ever wondered what those *ristras* are actually used for, you'll find out if you use the recipe for this dish. For dessert, an order of sweet, puffy Sopapillas drenched with honey and butter cooled any remaining embers.

Granted, the authentic Mexican dishes have attracted a strong and faithful following for the restaurant, but the activity on the patio places Los Olivos in a class by itself. Live music, mostly Latino, is offered nightly in this spacious room, which features a retractable roof, illuminated stained-glass windows, and a large mask with blinking eyes. The lively music and carnival atmosphere delight the crowds that flock to the patio on weekends to feast, mingle, and dance the night away, recreating a scene that first took place at this restaurant more than a half century ago.

Los Olivos' Mexican Rice

1 tablespoon cooking oil	½ medium bell pepper, chopped
1 cup long grain rice	½ teaspoon salt
1 clove garlic, minced	¼ teaspoon pepper
½ medium onion, chopped	½ cup tomato sauce
½ medium tomato, chopped	3 cups chicken broth

Heat oil in dutch oven over medium-high heat. Add rice and sauté until golden brown. Add garlic, onion, tomato, bell pepper, salt, and pepper. Sauté for 1 to 2 minutes. Add tomato sauce and chicken broth and bring to boiling stage. Reduce heat to lowest setting, cover pot, and cook for 10 minutes. Remove from heat. Allow pot to stand, covered, for 20 minutes. Season with salt and pepper if desired. Makes 3½ cups.

Los Olivos' Sonora Enchiladas

Red Chile Sauce

10 dried red chilies
water for boiling
4 tablespoons shortening

2 cloves garlic, minced
1½ tablespoons flour
½ tablespoon salt

Remove stems and seeds from red chilies. Boil chilies in enough water to cover, about 4 cups, for approximately 15 minutes or until chilies are tender. Remove from heat and let stand until cool enough to touch. Pour chilies and liquid into blender container and purée. Heat shortening in saucepan over medium-high heat. Add garlic and cook until light brown. Add flour and stir constantly until browned. Add salt and chile purée. Simmer and stir until thickened. If sauce gets too thick, add water to thin to desired consistency. Makes about 2½ cups.

Enchiladas

2 pounds corn masa
½ pound cheddar or longhorn
  cheese, shredded
1½ tablespoons salt
1 tablespoon baking powder
1 cup instant mashed
  potato flakes

2 cups water
oil for frying
2 cups shredded cheese
2 cups green onions, chopped
shredded lettuce
chopped tomato
sliced black olives

In large bowl, mix corn masa, cheddar or longhorn cheese, salt, baking powder, instant mashed potato flakes, and water together into a rough dough. Knead a few times to soften. Separate dough into 6 or 8 balls. Flatten balls with hands or rolling pin into patties about ½-inch thick. Heat 1 inch of oil in skillet. Place patties in oil, one at a time, and cook until both sides are golden brown. Add more oil to pan as needed. Drain patties on paper towels. Place each patty on ovenproof serving plate and cover with red chile sauce. Sprinkle shredded cheese and chopped onion over top of patty and put in hot oven until cheese is melted. Top with lettuce, tomato, and olive slices before serving. Serves 6 to 8.

P. Faires

Reata Pass Steakhouse

27500 North Alma School Parkway
SCOTTSDALE

The origin of the Reata Pass Steakhouse dates back to the 1880s, a time when stagecoaches rumbled across Arizona on dusty trails under a hot desert sun. Relief stations along the way offered cool drinks and hot meals to weary travelers and provided a place to water exhausted horses. According to legend, in 1882, a stagecoach stop was erected along the trail that ran between Phoenix and Fort McDowell, an army outpost established to protect

5:00 P.M. until 10:00 P.M.
Monday through Friday

Noon until 11:00 P.M.
Saturday

Noon until 10:00 P.M.
Sunday

For reservations
call (602) 585-7277

travelers from Apache Indian attacks. This stop was located at Reata Pass and offered support and sustenance to travelers faced with a two-thousand-foot climb through the nearby McDowell Mountains, no small feat for a rickety stage.

The stagecoach era ended long ago, but at Reata Pass the century-old tradition of feeding travelers has been preserved. Hefty, two-pound steaks, like the ones served in 1882, are still offered to passersby, who now arrive in sleek automobiles instead of stagecoaches. Part of the old stagecoach stop's original adobe wall remains in the restaurant's facade, which resembles a Western movie set.

As the years passed, settlers moved into the area and created the towns of Scottsdale, Carefree, and Paradise Valley. Modern transportation puts these towns only minutes away from Reata Pass. New dining rooms, added as the need appeared, have resulted in a sprawling complex with a seating capacity of two thousand.

Dining is available indoors—in rooms featuring Western antiques, wooden picnic-style tables, and a bar with sawdust floors—or under the stars on a spacious patio that remains open all year. Many prefer the desert setting on the patio, the best place for viewing the spectacular Arizona sunsets. More than a restaurant, the steakhouse offers a variety of entertainment including staged gunfights, live country-western music, and boot-stomping dances. But what the crowd really wants when they mosey on out to Reata Pass is what the stagecoach passengers wanted a hundred years ago, some tasty vittles!

The newspaper-style menu features typical steakhouse fare with a few surprises. The Rattlesnake Bites, an appetizer that looks and tastes like fried chicken, usually draws a few raised eyebrows. They are served with ranch dressing or barbecue sauce. But, the undisputed star attractions are the steaks, broiled over mesquite wood and served in sizes ranging from a 32-ounce grand porterhouse to an 8-ounce filet mignon. Ribs, chicken, and pork chops, also mesquite-smoked, are served with the standard dinner accompaniments—salad, cowboy beans, and corn on the cob. This restaurant wisely realizes that meaty cowboy-and-cowgirl fare isn't for everyone, so lighter dishes, like a catch of the day and chicken salad, are also available. The hot Deep-Dish Apple Pie smothered with cinnamon-laced ice cream is the favorite choice for dessert.

Reata Pass Steakhouse's Rattlesnake Bites

1 rattlesnake, skinned
½ cup cornmeal
¼ cup flour
salt and pepper
1 egg
½ cup milk
½ cup cooking oil
½ bottle ranch
  salad dressing

Cut snake into 4 pieces and debone. In bowl, combine cornmeal with flour, and salt and pepper. In another bowl, combine egg and milk, blending well. Roll snake pieces in cornmeal-flour mixture and then dip into egg-milk mix. Dredge in cornmeal-flour mixture again. Sauté in hot oil until browned on all sides. Serve with ranch dressing. Makes 2 appetizer servings.

Reata Pass Steakhouse's Barbecued Ribs

4 pounds beef or pork ribs
1 large onion, sliced
1 bay leaf
2 cloves
1 teaspoon salt
1 bottle (12 ounces)
  hickory-flavored
  barbecue sauce

Place ribs in large kettle and cover with water. Add onion, bay leaf, cloves, and salt. Bring to boil over high heat. Cover and reduce heat to simmer. Cook for 1 to 1½ hours until meat is tender. Remove ribs from water. Brush each side of ribs generously with barbecue sauce. Place in glass baking dish and cover with foil, but do not allow foil to touch meat. Refrigerate two hours or overnight. Grill 6 inches from coals. Turn and baste frequently with remaining barbecue sauce for 15 to 20 minutes, or until nicely browned. Serves 4.

Reata Pass Steakhouse's Barbecued Beans

1 pound small navy beans
1 medium onion, sliced
4 cups water
¼ cup packed brown sugar
  (optional)

1 teaspoon salt
⅛ teaspoon pepper
1 bottle commercial
  hickory-flavored
  barbecue sauce

Place beans and onions in large pan. Cover with water and bring to a boil. Reduce heat and simmer slowly for 2 to 3 hours until beans are tender. In small bowl, combine brown sugar, salt, pepper, and barbecue sauce. Stir sauce mixture into beans and simmer for 15 minutes. Serves 6.

Rusty Spur Saloon and Cafe

7245 East Main Street
OLD TOWN SCOTTSDALE

The first time I visited the Rusty Spur Saloon and Cafe in Old Town Scottsdale, tired horses were tied up outside the front door, while inside, a rambunctious standing-room-only crowd jostled for space. The noisy celebration was for the two-hundred-mile pony-express ride from Holbrook to

11:00 A.M. until 4:00 P.M.
Daily

For more information
call (602) 941-2628

Scottsdale which had just been completed. The ride happens every year and launches the Parada Del Sol, Scottsdale's famous mid-winter festival—a two-week celebration of western events including a parade, mock gunfights, and a rodeo.

The Rusty Spur occupies a brick building that was constructed in 1921. The building originally housed the Farmers' State Bank, the first bank in Scottsdale. In 1933, during the Great Depression, the bank closed for a "bank holiday" and never reopened. Located in the heart of historic downtown Scottsdale, the structure served as the town's first chamber of commerce, first library, a currency exchange, and an insurance agency before a couple named Sparks purchased the building in the 1950s and converted it into a saloon and cafe.

The original exterior brick walls remain at the Rusty Spur, although wood panels and a porch overhang were added at the front to achieve a more western, "Old Town" appearance. The old vault, which once stored the bank's money, now holds liquor. The wagon-wheel chandelier hanging inside the saloon's one-room interior dates back to banking days. Seating is sparse at this restaurant, with only a dozen or so tables. Additional seating is provided by a row of stools at the bar that stretches more than half the width of the room. An old-fashioned jukebox pumps out country-western favorites, and every evening the small stage against the wall is used by local country-western entertainers to keep things lively. What little wall space the small room affords is covered with an assortment of western paraphernalia that keeps the tourists entertained.

During my initial visit, I barely found a place to stand, let alone eat. However, when I returned a few months later accompanied by my son, Justin, there was an empty table and plenty of breathing space. A giant, stuffed bull's head stared down at us from his perch above the jukebox as we scanned the menu, which is short and to the point. And the point here is buffalo, a meat considered more "heart-healthy" than beef due to its lower cholesterol and fat content. Buffalo appears in various forms on the limited menu, but a few other items were also listed: barbecued pork, beef burgers, chili, a chicken-filet sandwich, and nachos. However, we were curious about the buffalo and decided to give it a try. Justin's Buffalo Burger, which arrived smothered in green chilies and melted cheese and served with a pile of fries, was gone in a matter of minutes. My bowl of steaming Buffalo Chili was also tasty, but I swear I wouldn't have known I was eating ground buffalo instead of ground beef if I hadn't been told. A cowboy type seated nearby advised me of the fact that real cowboys prefer their buffalo with an ice cold beer.

Buffalo meat can be a hard-to-find item, although in the Phoenix area there are grocery stores that carry it on a regular basis and others that are willing to place a special order for it. Just to be on the safe side, I checked back in the Rusty Spur kitchen before leaving and was assured that beef performs equally well in the recipes listed below.

Rusty Spur Saloon and Cafe's Buffalo Chili

2 tablespoons vegetable oil
1 pound ground buffalo meat
    (ground beef may
    be substituted)
1 medium onion, finely chopped
1 small clove garlic, minced
2½ cups canned kidney beans,
    drained

1 quart tomato juice
1 tablespoon cornstarch
1½ teaspoons sugar
1 teaspoon chili powder
½ teaspoon paprika
1 teaspoon salt

Heat oil in heavy cooking pot over medium-high heat. Add meat, onions, and garlic and cook until meat is brown. Reduce heat to low setting and add kidney beans and tomato juice. In small container, combine cornstarch, sugar, chili powder, paprika, and salt. Add to chili pot. Simmer ingredients for one hour, stirring occasionally. Serves 4 to 6 generously.

½ pound tortilla chips
1 cup buffalo chili
  (see recipe on previous page)
¾ cup melted processed cheese
¼ cup black olives, sliced

¼ cup tomato, diced
¼ cup onions, diced
2 tablespoons sliced jalapenos
generous dollop sour cream

Spread tortilla chips on large serving plate. Add layer of heated chili, followed by layer of warm melted cheese. In order given, add black olives, tomatoes, onions, jalapenos, and sour cream. Serves 3 to 4.

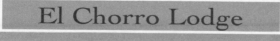

El Chorro Lodge

5550 East Lincoln Drive
PARADISE VALLEY

The El Chorro Lodge, one of the Scottsdale-area's oldest landmarks, was built at a time when many well-heeled easterners were enrolling their male offspring in the popular Judson School for Boys. Prominent families were attracted to the small, private college-preparatory school with its championship tennis and polo teams. In 1934, a satellite institution for girls was built nearby, but the Judson School for Girls never quite developed as planned. A few years later, the facilities of the girls' school were sold to a couple from Montana named Gruber. In 1937, this enterprising duo converted the complex of white stucco buildings with red-tile roofs into the El Chorro Lodge, and they continued its operation for thirty-six years.

Breakfast
9:00 A.M. until 3:00 P.M.
Saturday

Lunch
11:00 A.M. until 3:00 P.M.
Monday through Friday

9:00 A.M. until 3:00 P.M.
Saturday

Sunday Brunch
9:00 A.M. until 3:00 P.M.

Dinner
6:00 P.M. until 11:00 P.M.
Nightly

For reservations
(recommended)
call (602) 948-5170

News of the snug desert hideaway and the good food served there eventually spread to the Hollywood set, attracting celebrities to the pleasant lodge nestled between two mountains. Clark Gable, Milton Berle, and Sylvia Sidney came to stay and dine on the very same dishes that appear on the menu today. The original recipes are still used at the lodge, which was sold in 1973 to the Grubers's former employees, Joe and Evie Miller.

Although the restaurant expanded under the Millers's ownership and management, the relaxed charm of the original lodge has endured. It is most evident in the cozy lounge, which was the original schoolroom. With its old adobe walls and distinctive beehive fireplace, this longtime gathering spot for locals still looks much as it did in the 30s and 40s. The restaurant's unpretentious, rambling interior consists of five comfortable dining rooms which were added as needed. The overall effect is that of a casual, friendly private club featuring a southwestern decor of stucco walls and exposed over-head beams. Several pieces of interesting western art also add to the decor at the lodge. A particularly striking piece, a large metal sculp-ture of a cowboy on horseback, is located at the restaurant's entrance.

Warm winter temperatures and stunning mountain views make the outdoor patio a perfect place to enjoy one of the lodge's celebrated meals. My choice on a warm January afternoon was Beef Stroga-noff, made from a recipe handed down from the Grubers and still a favorite at the lodge. The dish of tender chunks of beef tenderloin served with buttery noodles was outstanding and a bit different from the usual due to its beefier sauce and the absence of mushrooms. The Rack of Lamb and the Chicken-Fried Steak are other dishes that have earned this restaurant a faithful following, and the legend-ary Sticky Buns and Eggs Benedict endure as star attractions at Sun-day brunch.

Not wanting to leave this lovely restaurant, or my place in the sun, I stalled for more time by ordering another historic item off the menu for dessert, the Ice Box Cake. Don't be fooled by the name of this dessert, made from another recipe handed down from the Gruber recipe collection. The delectable chocolate confection deserves a more distinguished title, but history dictates at this restaurant, so the name stays.

El Chorro Lodge's Beef Stroganoff

1½ pounds beef tenderloin
  or boneless sirloin
¼ to ½ teaspoon salt
¼ teaspoon black pepper
1 medium red onion, sliced
  into ½-inch-thick pieces
4 tablespoons butter or
  margarine

2 tablespoons flour
1 cup beef stock or beef broth
1 teaspoon Dijon-type
  mustard
¼ cup sour cream, room
  temperature

Trim visible fat from meat. Cut into 2- by ½-inch strips. Ar-range heavy brown paper on working surface. Spread meat strips onto paper and sprinkle evenly with salt and pepper. Toss and mix. Spread meat out again and top with onion slices. Let stand for approximately 2 hours at room temperature. Make sauce by melting 2 tablespoons of butter over low heat in a large heavy skillet. Add flour and blend. Add stock or broth. Mix and heat until thick, about 5 to 8 minutes. Add mustard and blend well. Remove sauce from heat. In second large skillet, melt remaining butter over medium-high heat. Add beef and onion slices. Cook quickly until brown, approximately 10 minutes. Remove and discard onions. Add browned beef to sauce. Cover and cook over low heat for 15 minutes, stirring once or twice. Remove from heat. Add sour cream, stir, and serve. Serves 4.

El Chorro Lodge's Ice Box Cake

8 ounces semi-sweet chocolate
3 tablespoons hot water
4 eggs, separated
2 tablespoons confectioners' sugar

4 ounces walnuts, chopped
8 ounces whipping cream
1 package ladyfingers

Melt chocolate and hot water in a double boiler. Remove from heat. Add egg yolks, one at a time, to melted chocolate and beat until smooth. In a separate small bowl, combine confectioners' sugar with walnuts and blend well. Add to egg-chocolate mixture. In separate bowl, whip egg whites until stiff. In another bowl, whip whipping cream until stiff. Fold egg whites gently into whipped cream, then add to chocolate mixture and fold gently until blended. Line an 8- by 12-inch dish with ladyfingers and pour mixture over top. Refrigerate for 12 to 24 hours. Cut into squares and serve with whipped cream. Serves 6 to 8.

Aunt Chilada's at Squaw Peak

7330 North Dreamy Draw Drive,
The Pointe Hilton Resort at Squaw Peak
PHOENIX

*I*t's hard to visualize Aunt Chilada's, a rambling stone-and-timber structure on the impeccably landscaped grounds of the Hilton's Pointe at Squaw Peak Resort, as an outpost in the wilderness. But when the building was erected back in the 1880s, this lush playground at the base of Squaw Peak Mountain was mostly barren desert with a scattering of cacti, tumbleweeds, and mercury mines.

11:00 A.M. until 10:00 P.M.
Sunday through Thursday

11:00 A.M. until 11:00 P.M.
Friday and Saturday

For reservations
call (602) 944-1286

Thousands of Santa Fe Railroad ties, bricks, and mortar—made from materials gathered in the area—were used to construct the building, which served as a general store and trading post for miners and their families. The building's address on Dreamy Draw Drive refers to the tipsy condition of the miners after working a shift in the toxic mines.

As mining operations ceased, the area developed commercially, and the old trading post adapted to new roles. In the 1930s, the building became a restaurant, saloon, and gas station. A decade later, it was converted into a Mexican restaurant. By the time a full century had taken its toll, the structure was in such a wretched state that demolition seemed the only answer.

Thanks to the Hilton's million-dollar restoration project, the century-old structure was rescued from the wrecking ball. Today, it is one of the area's largest and most interesting Mexican restaurants. It's obvious that architectural preservation was a priority during the renovation, as much of the original eight-thousand-square-foot structure looks the same as it did a century ago. The aged timbers and stone walls remain, as do the original rock fireplaces and the old smoker—still used to slow-cook meats at the restaurant.

The atmosphere at Aunt Chilada's is Old-World romantic, and you are under its spell before you even reach the front door of the restaurant. A covered walk dripping with bougainvillea vines leads past bubbling courtyard fountains to the entrance. Inside the sprawling structure, dining rooms, cantinas, and walled patios vibrate with the colorful sights and sounds of Mexico—a perfect setting for enjoying the restaurant's award-winning traditional Mexican cuisine.

A festive atmosphere does wonders for the appetite, and mine was in full bloom the day I dined at Aunt Chilada's. The Pechugas de Pollo, a delicious dish featuring breast of chicken wrapped in a flour tortilla and smothered in a zesty cheese sauce, lived up to its excellent reputation and my expectations. For my indecisive dining companions, nothing else would do but "The Whole Aunt Chilada." This generous sampler of the restaurant's most popular items is just the thing to feed a band of hungry gringos, which, judging from the scene at our table, is exactly what it did. Another item worth noting is the tasty Fideo, an interesting noodle side dish. It was a pleasant change from rice and refried beans, the standard accompaniment at most Mexican restaurants.

You won't want to skip dessert, especially after indulging in one of the chef's fiery specialties. Deep-Fried Ice Cream and smooth-as-silk Flan will put out any smoldering embers, and puffy Sopapillas leave the sweetest aftertaste. Don't be surprised if, after dessert, you're still not ready to leave this charming restaurant. If you have time to linger, there's a colorful Mexican gift shop near the entrance that's perfect for browsing.

Aunt Chilada's at Squaw Peak's Pechuga de Pollo

2½ pounds chicken breasts, boneless and skinless
½ teaspoon salt
½ teaspoon paprika
½ teaspoon white pepper
2 tablespoons butter

6 cups chili con queso sauce (recipe follows)
6 flour tortillas, 13-inch size
⅔ cup Monterey Jack cheese, grated
¾ cup cheddar cheese, grated

Cut chicken breasts into strips. In medium bowl, combine chicken with salt, paprika, and white pepper. In large skillet or Dutch oven, melt butter over medium-high heat. Add chicken strips and sauté until lightly browned, approximately 3 to 4 minutes. Reduce heat and add chili con queso sauce. Stir and cook for about 3 minutes. Remove chicken from sauce with tongs. Lay tortillas flat and place ½ to ¾ cup chicken into center of each tortilla. Roll into burros. Place burros in large, flat casserole dish. Pour remaining sauce from skillet over burros. Top with cheeses. Bake in 450-degree oven about 4 minutes until cheese is melted. Serves 6.

Aunt Chilada's at Squaw Peak's Del Norte Chili Con Queso Sauce

3 cups quality commercial
  green chili sauce
1 cup sour cream
³/4 cup Monterey Jack cheese,
  grated
³/4 cup cheddar cheese, grated
¹/3 cup half-and-half

3 fresh jalapeno chilies,
  seeded and sliced
6 mild green chilies, seeded
  and cut into strips

Combine all ingredients in saucepan. Cook and stir over low heat until cheese is melted. Makes approximately 6 cups.

Aunt Chilada's at Squaw Peak's Fideo

6 tablespoons lard
1 pound vermicelli
  fideo noodles, crushed
3 cups beef stock or beef broth
4 cups water
½ cup tomato purée
¾ teaspoon granulated garlic
1 tablespoon salt

¹/3 cup medium red pepper,
  julienne sliced
¹/3 cup medium green pepper,
  julienne sliced
¹/2 cup yellow onion, diced
1 cup tomatoes, diced
1 cup frozen peas, thawed

Melt lard in large skillet. Add noodles and brown. In another saucepan, combine beef stock, water, tomato purée, garlic, and salt. Bring to boil. Add peppers, onion, and tomatoes to noodles. Add hot broth and stir. Boil for 5 minutes or until liquid is completely absorbed. Turn off heat, cover, and let stand for 15 minutes. Stir in thawed peas, allow to stand for a few minutes until peas are thoroughly warmed. Serves 4 to 6.

Carriage House

115 North Sixth Street (center of Heritage Square)
PHOENIX

9:00 A.M. until 4:00 P.M.
Monday through Saturday

2:00 P.M. until 4:00 P.M.
Sunday

For information
call (602) 495-1997

Whenever I approach downtown Phoenix, the state capital and the nation's eighth-largest city, I mentally prepare myself for the sleek high rises that sparkle like diamonds in the intense midday sun. In this sprawling metropolis, anything constructed in the 1920s and 1930s is considered historic. That is why I was surprised at discovering Heritage Square, an entire city block containing structures from the late 1800s. This lone remaining cluster of residential buildings from the original townsite of Phoenix has been preserved as a city park and cultural center and is listed on the National Register of Historic Places.

At Heritage Square, it doesn't seem to matter that the city's pulse ticks nearby. In this charming, turn-of-the-twentieth-century setting complete with flower gardens and old-time lampposts, you'll be transported back to the days when the pace was slower and lunch was a lingering affair.

In the center of the square is the Carriage House, a bakery and sandwich shop located in a historic brick building that once served as a mule barn. It was constructed in 1899 by cattleman and flour miller, Leon Bouvier, who built the two-story barn behind his midwestern-style brick bungalow. The sturdy, gable-roofed structure was used to house animals, vehicles, harnesses, and the groom, who reportedly lived in the loft above his keep. In 1911, Bouvier sold the bungalow and barn to Eliza Teeter. After renting the property to a succession of tenants, Mrs. Teeter eventually moved into the bungalow and remained until her death at the age of ninety-six.

Today, you'll find no carriages or mules inside the Carriage House. The stables have been replaced with a serving counter, cold-drink case, and a kitchen that creates delicious fresh-baked breads, desserts, and an assortment of breakfast and luncheon dishes prepared from recipes dating back to the early 1900s. A blackboard near the large, double doors—wide enough to allow easy passage for a carriage—announces the menu, which changes daily and features the foods of the season. Because space is at a premium inside the former barn, dining is outdoors at umbrella-covered tables completely encircling the building.

Luckily for me, the day I visited the Carriage House the menu featured Chimichangas, tasty meat-filled tortillas fried to a golden brown. A fruit salad and Fresh Peach Cobbler were also featured that day. My leisurely midday repast was enhanced by my view of Heritage Square's oldest and newest buildings—the meticulously restored Rosson House, an elegant 1895 Victorian home that was considered to be one of the city's most prominent homes in the late 1800s, and the Lath House Pavilion, a contemporary structure completed in 1980. It was no surprise to learn that this impressive outdoor pavilion, combining nineteenth-century concepts of a botanical conservatory, gazebo, beer garden, and pedestrian shopping arcade, is a popular site for many city-coordinated events and private gatherings.

As I walked back to my car and, once again, experienced the noise and accelerated tempo of contemporary urban life, I applauded this city's spirit of preservation and the operators of the Carriage House, Mary Kay Myers and her family, for providing a relaxing and enjoyable visit to the turn of the century. Even if the visit was a brief one.

Carriage House's Flour Tortillas

4 cups all-purpose flour　　*½ cup shortening*
2 teaspoons salt　　　　　　*1½ cups warm water*

Combine flour and salt together in mixing bowl. Cut shortening into flour mixture with fingers until mixture resembles coarse meal. Add warm water and mix until dough is soft and somewhat sticky. Place on floured board and knead until dough is soft and springy and holds its shape. Divide dough into 20 equal portions, about the size of large eggs. Pat by hand on floured board and flatten into 6- or 7-inch circles, or roll each ball with rolling pin into paper-thin, 8- to 10-inch circles. Heat a heavy ungreased griddle or skillet over medium-high heat. Cook each tortilla until bubbles form and brown flecks appear, about 1 to 2 minutes on each side. Stack each tortilla between layers of waxed paper and cover with a towel until ready to serve. Tortillas can be buttered and eaten alone, like a slice of bread, or filled with shredded meat, chili, or beans and folded into a roll to form a burro. When a meat-filled burro is fried in hot oil until golden brown, it's called a chimichanga. Makes 20 tortillas.

Carriage House's Fresh Peach Cobbler

2 cups flour
1 teaspoon salt
2/3 cup shortening
6 tablespoons ice water

7 to 8 fresh peaches,
   peeled and sliced
3/4 cup sugar

Make cobbler crust by combining flour with salt in mixing bowl. Work shortening into flour mixture with fingers until well mixed. Add ice water, a tablespoon at a time, mixing until a soft, easily handled dough is formed. Divide dough in half and place on a floured board. Use a floured rolling pin to roll dough into two 9-inch squares. Line the bottom of a square 9-inch pan with one crust. Cover crust with sliced peaches. Sprinkle sugar evenly over fruit and cover with remaining crust. Set oven to 350 degrees and bake for approximately 45 minutes to 1 hour, until top of crust is golden brown. Remove from oven and allow cobbler to sit until fruit thickens, about 15 to 20 minutes. Makes 4 to 6 servings.

Goldie's 1895 House

362 North Second Avenue
PHOENIX

$\mathcal{A}$n old Victorian home is a rare sight in modern metropolitan Phoenix. That is why I felt as if I had discovered a precious jewel when I arrived at Goldie's 1895 House. This historic restaurant is a gem, inside and out.

The stately, two-story structure, built of sand brick in 1895, is considered the oldest Victorian house in Phoenix. A mystery surrounds the identity of the original owners, a result, some say, of the home's former role as a bordello. The house changed hands many times throughout its history—serving as a residence, boarding house, and hotel. In 1976, the building was renovated into a restaurant. The current owner, Goldie Burge, who purchased the restaurant in 1989, has cleverly transformed the century-old house into a unique Victorian showplace by adding a gallery, museum, and a dinner theater.

The nostalgia at this gingerbread-trimmed house will sweep you away. The building overflows with interesting antiques, both indoors and outside on the garden patio. The Victorian style is apparent throughout the interior, which features the original wood moldings, floors, and fireplaces. The dramatic effects of creative restoration are evident in many areas. The most spectacular example is the soaring redwood ceiling that replaced the original attic and now dominates the spacious upstairs dining room. It is said that more than five miles of redwood boards were used to cover the exposed attic ceiling. The attic's old floorboards have been cleverly reworked into tabletops, allowing diners to literally eat off the floors.

The charming decor of this one-of-a-kind restaurant is matched by its imaginative cuisine. Traditional American and continental dishes appear on the menu, but in the turn-of-the-century environment at

Lunch
11:00 A.M. until 2:00 P.M.
Monday through Friday

Dinner
5:00 P.M. until 9:00 P.M.
Monday through Thursday

5:00 P.M. until 10:00 P.M.
Friday and Saturday

3:30 P.M. until 9:00 P.M.
Sunday

Brunch
11:00 A.M. until 3:00 P.M.
Sunday

For reservations
(recommended)
call (602) 254-0338

this restaurant, expect some interesting Victorian enhancements. Deciding on an entrée is no easy feat when faced with such items as Medallions of Beef poached in Wine and Garlic Sauce, or Capered Chicken flambéed in Brandy Sauce. Finally, I chose the chicken and followed the menu's suggested wine, a white zinfandel.

My meal was everything I had hoped it would be—beautifully presented, graciously served, and delicious. Alas, what was I to do but finish everything set before me? The result was having to pass up one of the chef's celebrated desserts. However, I definitely will save room next time. My return trip to the Goldie's 1895 House will include dinner theater upstairs, where I plan to eat off the floors.

Goldie's 1895 House's Capered Chicken

¼ cup unsalted butter
¼ cup flour
1½ cups beef stock or bouillon
½ cup dry white wine
1 tablespoon capers in
   2 tablespoons juice
¼ cup half-and-half
¼ cup whipping cream,
   room temperature
a dash of white pepper

4 chicken breasts,
   boneless and skinless
4 tablespoons butter,
   lightly salted
3 tablespoons garlic, minced
2 cloves shallots, minced
3 ounces brandy
½ cup green onions,
   finely chopped
1 cup fresh mushrooms, sliced

In saucepan, prepare roux by melting unsalted butter over low heat. Gradually add flour, stirring or whisking until mixture is smooth and thick. Remove from heat and set aside. In medium saucepan, bring beef stock or bouillon to boil. Add wine, capers, and caper juice. When mixture returns to boiling point, remove from heat and set aside. When cool, add half-and-half, whipping cream, and pepper. Gently add cream mixture into roux, blending over very low heat until smooth and mixture has thickened. Remove from heat and set aside.

Pound chicken breasts to flatten. In large skillet or sauté pan, melt 2 tablespoons lightly salted butter over low heat. Add 1 tablespoon garlic, shallots, and chicken. Braise chicken on both sides until evenly browned. Pour 2 ounces of warm brandy over chicken and flame. When flame has burned off, cover and simmer until chicken is cooked, approximately 6 to 10 minutes.

While chicken is cooking, melt remaining 2 tablespoons lightly salted butter in large sauté pan over medium heat. Add onions, sliced mushrooms, and remaining garlic. Sauté until tender. Stir caper-mushroom sauce into mushroom mixture. Add remaining ounce of brandy. Flame and set aside. Remove chicken from pan and keep warm. Add liquid remaining in pan to caper-mushroom sauce, stirring over low heat until ingredients are well blended and thoroughly warmed. Pour equal amount of warm sauce over each chicken breast and serve. Serves 4.

Goldie's 1895 House's Sautéed Shrimp with Red Pepper Sauce

3 cups chicken broth
4 tablespoons unsalted butter
½ cup onion, chopped
½ cup celery, chopped
1 small green pepper, diced small
1 large red pepper, diced small
½ teaspoon freshly ground black pepper
¼ cup fresh parsley, chopped

1 cup heavy cream
1½ tablespoons cornstarch
¼ cup cold water
1 pound large tiger shrimp, peeled and deveined
1 pound cheese-stuffed tortellini, cooked and drained
chopped fresh parsley and Parmesan cheese for garnish

In medium saucepan, bring chicken broth to a slow boil. In a sauté pan, heat 2 tablespoons butter over low heat until melted. Add onion, celery, green pepper, and half of the red pepper. Sauté until the vegetables are soft, approximately 2 minutes. Add vegetables to boiling broth. Reduce heat and simmer for 60 minutes. Remove from heat and pour broth through sieve, straining off cooked vegetables. Discard strained vegetables and return broth to pan. Bring to a slow boil. Add black pepper, parsley, remaining red pepper, and cream. In small bowl or cup, blend cornstarch with water until smooth. Add to hot broth and stir until mixture thickens. In a sauté pan, melt remaining 2 tablespoons butter over medium heat. Add shrimp and sauté for about 5 minutes until done, stirring constantly. Divide prepared pasta into 4 servings. Top each serving with equal amounts of shrimp and top with red pepper cream sauce. Garnish with additional chopped parsley and Parmesan cheese. Serves 4.

Los Dos Molinos

8646 South Central Avenue
PHOENIX

In a city where so-called "South-of-the-Border" food is as common as cactus, discovering a restaurant that sets your taste buds dancing with robust chile-spiked dishes is a noteworthy event. Authentic, fiery New Mexican dishes are the passion and pride of the kitchen at Los Dos Molinos, a colorful old adobe home located in south Phoenix.

The house was built in 1909 and once belonged to silent-screen cowboy Tom Mix. In 1990, the Chavez family purchased the structure and spent eighteen months restoring and redecorating the restaurant. To give the restaurant a festive atmosphere, they added tabletops tiled in neon yellow and blue, brightly painted booths, lots of funky folk art, and Christmas lights that twinkle all year. The restaurant's numerous awards have been framed and hang behind the counter near the front door, where you'll also find a collection of Chavez-family photos.

A walled courtyard at the front of the restaurant provides a pleasant area to wait for the exciting, spicy fare that has earned this restaurant a large following. But don't be fooled by the cool white exterior of the courtyard. Inside, the heat is on, and gringos with sensitive palates should be aware. After all, the restaurant is named for the two mills, *los dos molinos*, that grind the hot New Mexican chilies responsible for the fire in the food served here. Even the restaurant's business card claims "Some Like It Hot." Judging from the usual mob waiting to get inside, the card is an understatement. To make the waiting less painful, a gift shop is located off the courtyard.

Upon being seated, an iced pitcher of water is delivered to your table along with a heaping bowl of warm tortilla chips and salsa. The water is a necessity if you intend to dip a chip. There are those who will argue that the green salsa is hotter than the red, but each one packs a punch. The salsa should give you a clue about how much heat you can handle. If you are in doubt about what to order, friendly

11:00 A.M. until 9:00 P.M.
Tuesday through Saturday

11:00 A.M. until 8:00 P.M.
Sunday

No reservations are taken.
For information
call (602) 243-9113

servers will help you choose a dish with the proper temperature. A simple, double-sided menu lists a variety of Mexican combination plates and à la carte items, all equally delicious. All the familiar Mexican favorites are listed — enchiladas, chimichangas, rellenos, tostadas, and tamales — along with the specialties of the house.

Before I ordered, I overheard a server at the next table recommend the Flautas dinner, a plateful of deep-fried tortilla rolls filled with shredded beef or chicken and served with sour cream and guacamole, to a young woman seeking something on the milder side. But throwing caution to the wind, I ordered the Carne Adovada Burro along with a Raspberry Iced Tea. Granted, the tender chunks of pork marinated in red chilies and tucked inside a soft tortilla blanket did leave my tongue tingling and my forehead dripping, but the taste was well worth it. For dessert, a Sopapilla, a puffy tortilla pillow sprinkled with honey, cinnamon, and sugar, put out the fire very nicely.

Los Dos Molinos' Carne Adovada

5 pounds pork loin	½ cup white onion, chopped
1 cup all-purpose flour	1 head fresh garlic, peeled
salt and pepper	1½ cups water, or beef or
1 to 2 tablespoons cooking oil	chicken broth
8 dried red chile pods	

Trim fat from pork and cut meat into 2-inch cubes. In paper bag, combine flour and meat together with desired amount of salt and pepper. Shake until meat is well covered. Heat oil in heavy skillet until sizzling. Add pork pieces. Cook and stir for 1 to 2 minutes until browned. Remove from heat. Remove stems and seeds from chile pods and chop into pieces. Place chile pieces into blender container. Add chopped onion. Separate garlic into cloves and dice. Add to blender. Pour broth or water into blender container and blend for 1 or 2 minutes. Place pork pieces in ovenproof pan or baking dish. Pour chile mixture over meat and bake in 300-degree oven for 1 to 2 hours, or until meat is tender and juicy. Serve with warm tortillas. Serves 8 to 10.

Los Dos Molinos' Green Chile

1 teaspoon cooking oil
1 cup lean pork, cut
   into 1-inch cubes
1 cup lean beef, cut
   into 1-inch cubes
¼ cup white onion, chopped
12 long green chilies,
   roasted and peeled

½ head garlic,
   peeled and minced
2 cups broth, beef or chicken
½ teaspoon pepper
½ teaspoon salt

Heat cooking oil to sizzling point in large heavy skillet. Add meat cubes and onion. Toss lightly until meat is browned and onions are tender. Remove from heat and set aside. Chop chilies and place in medium bowl. (Chile oil can burn sensitive tissues, so be careful to never touch your eyes or mouth when working with fresh chilies.) Add garlic, broth, and seasonings to chilies. Reheat meat in heavy skillet over low heat. Add chile-broth mixture, stirring well. Bring to a boil then reduce heat and simmer for an additional 30 minutes. Serves 3 to 4.

P·Faires

Orangerie At The Arizona Biltmore

24th Street and Missouri Avenue
PHOENIX

The Phoenix area has long been a mecca for winter sun seekers, and it is well-known for its abundance of elegant resorts. The historic Arizona Biltmore, which houses the Orangerie, is one of the most famous. With over sixty-five years of tradition behind it, the "Jewel of the Desert" has carved its name deep into the Arizona landscape.

The resort, whose design was inspired by consulting architect Frank Lloyd Wright, was constructed in 1929 of pre-cast concrete blocks molded on site and cast with exquisite detail and patterns. In 1930, the unique hotel was purchased by Chicago chewing-gum magnate, William Wrigley, Jr. During the forty-four years of Wrigley-family ownership, the hotel gained international prominence as a luxury resort. That reputation has endured throughout a succession of owners and numerous renovations. Today, the Arizona Biltmore, nestled in the foothills of Squaw Peak on thirty-six acres of landscaped gardens, remains the grande dame of Arizona resorts.

For more than six decades, the luxurious resort has pampered the rich and famous, many of whom left lasting memories at the hotel. Martha Raye reportedly fancied lawn games, while Edna Ferber wrote novels during her stay. Presidents Gerald Ford, George Bush, and Bill Clinton have all been guests, and President Ronald Reagan and his wife, Nancy, spent their honeymoon here. Another honeymooning couple, the zany Harpo Marx and his bride, are said to have caused quite a stir by holding hands and skipping around the formal dining room after meals. However, it's possible this display was simply an enthusiastic response to the Orangerie's celebrated cuisine.

Located off the spacious lobby in the resort's main building, the Orangerie owes its stunning contemporary decor to a recent renovation project. A warm shade of yellow appears on the upholstered

Lunch
11:30 A.M. until 2:30 P.M.
Monday through Friday

Dinner
6:00 P.M. until 11:00 P.M.
Monday through Saturday

Sunday Brunch
10:00 A.M. until 2:30 P.M.

Jackets required for men.

For reservations
(required)
call (602) 954-2507

chairs and in the printed carpeting, adding a soft touch to the restaurant's awesome and somewhat austere interior.

From my seat overlooking a manicured putting green, I watched golfers practicing their strokes in the January afternoon sun. A polished waiter bearing an extensive wine list and luncheon menu suggested a crisp Chardonnay and the Pepper-Seared Ahi Tuna. As soon as the entrée arrived, I knew immediately why this restaurant continues to win prestigious culinary awards. The tower of tuna medallions and tomatoes, garnished with red pepper twirls, lemon zests, and fresh rosemary skewers and served with ravioli and potato crisps, was an artistic masterpiece, a feast for the eyes as well as the palate. My dining companion's choice, a Skillet Seared Breast of Pheasant, followed suit. We both agreed that whenever we need some pampering, we'll reserve a table at the elegant Orangerie.

Orangerie at the Arizona Biltmore's Skillet-Seared Breast of Pheasant

1 spaghetti squash
salt, pepper, and nutmeg
   to taste
1 pound parsnips, pared
   and quartered
1 cup milk
½ cup heavy cream
1 pound cranberries
1 cup water
1 cup sugar
1 orange, peeled and sliced

a dash of nutmeg
4 breasts of pheasant,
   8 ounces each
½ cup plus 2 tablespoons
   peanut oil
½ cup all-purpose flour
3 garlic heads, peeled
3 to 4 fresh parsley stems
2¾ cups white wine
6 tablespoons butter

Split spaghetti squash in 2 pieces and spoon out seeds and excess fibers. Lightly butter and season with salt and pepper. Bake in 350-degree oven for 1 hour until cooked through. When cool, use fork to remove squash from skin in spaghetti-like strings. Set aside. Poach parsnips in milk over medium heat until tender, about 20 minutes. Strain and season with salt, pepper, and nutmeg. Add cream and parsnip purée in food processor or blender. Set aside. In separate pan, bring cranberries, water, sugar, orange slices, and dash of nutmeg to boil. Reduce heat to low, cover, and simmer for 40 minutes. Set aside.

Debone pheasant breasts. Prepare stock by browning carcasses in ½ cup peanut oil in stock pot. Add flour and continue to brown. Split garlic heads and add to stock with parsley stems and wine. Season with salt and pepper and boil for 3 minutes. Add enough cold water to cover and bring to another boil. Lower heat and simmer for 2 to 3 hours. Strain, return to pot, and reduce by ⅓ in volume. In ovenproof pan over high heat, heat 1 tablespoon butter and remaining 2 tablespoons peanut oil. Add pheasant pieces and sear on all sides. Remove pan to 350-degree oven and allow to finish cooking for 30 minutes until breasts are tender. In sauté pan, melt 2 tablespoons butter over medium heat. Add squash and cook over low heat until hot. Mix 2 teaspoons cranberry sauce with 1 cup pheasant stock and remaining 3 tablespoons butter to make cranberry-stock sauce. Strain and season to taste. Divide squash, parsnip purée, and pheasant into four equal portions. Serve with cranberry-stock sauce. Serves 4.

Orangerie at the Arizona Biltmore's Pepper-Seared Ahi Tuna

2 pounds Ahi tuna
salt and coarsely ground
pepper to taste
4 tomatoes, yellow preferred
½ cup fresh basil, chopped
½ cup whipping cream
½ cup fresh parsley

1 tablespoon minced garlic
½ ounce ground almonds
olive oil
lemon zest, red pepper, and
fresh rosemary skewers for
garnish

Cut tuna into medallions and season with pepper and salt. Skin and dice tomatoes and sauté in small pan. Season with salt and pepper, add ¼ cup basil, and set aside. Prepare pesto sauce by simmering whipping cream over medium heat until reduced by ⅔. Mix in parsley, remaining ¼ cup basil, garlic, and almonds. Mix gently and strain. Set aside. Sauté tuna medallions in olive oil over high heat for approximately 2 minutes on each side until done. In serving plate, alternate layers of tuna with tomato mixture to form stacks. Top with pesto sauce and garnish with lemon zests, red pepper twirls, and rosemary skewers. Serves 6.

The Terrace Dining Room
At The Wigwam Resort

300 West Indian School Road
LITCHFIELD PARK

It's hard to believe that the celebrated Wigwam Resort, which houses the elegant Terrace Dining Room, owes its existence to an ordinary, old rubber tire. However, back in 1915, that tire was neither ordinary or old. At that time, Paul Litchfield, a vice-president of the Goodyear Tire and Rubber Company, developed a revolutionary design for a heavy-duty tire that was more durable than other tires on the market. Production of the tire required a particular cotton that was becoming difficult to obtain during World War I. Arizona's climate seemed ideal for growing the cotton, so in 1916, Goodyear

Breakfast
6:30 A.M. until 10:30 A.M.
Daily

Lunch
11:30 A.M. until 2:00 P.M.
Daily

Dinner
5:00 P.M. until 10:00 P.M.
Daily
Jacket and tie required for men.

For reservations
(recommended)
call (602) 935-3811

began growing the plant along the Agua Fria River. This marked the beginning of a cotton-growing venture that would eventually expand into a thirty-eight-thousand-acre empire named Litchfield Park.

In 1919, a two-story adobe structure was built to house and feed Goodyear Tire and Rubber Company executives and visitors at Litchfield Park. Dubbed "the Wigwam," the house remained a private operation until 1929, when it was opened to the public as The Wigwam Resort. For thirty years, the facility continued to expand, and it eventually became known as one of the Southwest's leading resorts. In 1986, the 463-acre resort was acquired by SunCor Development Company, which began a major, forty-five-million-dollar refurbishment that was completed in 1991.

The original territorial style has been preserved throughout the elegant low-rise resort, which continues to earn prestigious Mobil Five-Star Awards year after year. The decor reflects cowboy and Indian influences, taking the visitor back to the turn of the twentieth century when Arizona was still a territory.

Of the resort's three restaurants, the Terrace Dining Room is the oldest and the most formal. Muted shades of lavender, turquoise, and sand flow throughout the large room, which has been cleverly divided into three dining areas. The pale adobe walls make an inviting backdrop for the refined interior.

The same continental and American dishes that have pleased discriminating palates for over sixty-five years are still served at the restaurant, although many have been updated and now reflect the flavors of the Southwest. The executive chef practiced his culinary wizardry at the White House during the Reagan administration, so I paid close attention when he recommended the Black Bean Soup for an appetizer. This flavorful soup, garnished with sour cream, cilantro, and lime, arrived with strips of tri-colored tortillas festively arranged around the bowl. My entrée, the Medallions of Venison Loin with Cherry Sauce and Lentil Ragout, was another of the chef's suggestions and proved to be equally outstanding. Each delicious morsel confirmed this historic resort's award-winning reputation.

The Terrace Dining Room at the Wigwam Resort's Black Bean Soup

½ pound black beans
¼ cup bacon strips, diced
¼ cup onion, diced
2 teaspoons minced garlic
¼ cup celery, diced
¼ cup carrots, diced
2 tablespoons port wine
2 quarts chicken stock, or broth
2 quarts ham stock
½ cup tomato purée

½ bunch fresh cilantro, chopped
¼ teaspoon thyme
¼ teaspoon dry mustard
¼ teaspoon ground black pepper
1 teaspoon cumin powder
½ chipotle chile, minced
sour cream and fresh cilantro for garnish

Rinse black beans thoroughly, cover with cold water, and soak overnight. In large soup pot, sauté bacon with onions, garlic, celery, and carrots until nicely browned. Add drained beans, port wine, chicken and ham stocks, tomato purée, cilantro, thyme, pepper, mustard, pepper, cumin powder, and chile. Bring soup to a boil. Reduce heat to low and simmer, covered, until beans are tender, about 45 minutes. Garnish top of each soup portion with ¼ teaspoon of sour cream and fresh cilantro. Makes approximately 2½ quarts. Serves 8 to 10.

The Terrace Dining Room at the Wigwam Resort's Medallions of Venison Loin with Cherry Sauce and Lentil Ragout

8 venison loin medallions
  (3 ounces each)
salt and pepper
3 tablespoons corn oil
1 slice bacon, diced
¼ cup leeks, white part only,
  diced
¼ cup carrots, diced
2 shallots, minced
1 teaspoon fresh garlic, minced

⅛ cup white wine
1 thyme sprig
1 bay leaf
1 teaspoon fresh lime juice
3 ounces (about ⅓ cup)
  yellow lentils
3 ounces (about ⅓ cup)
  pink lentils
1 cup chicken stock

Season venison with salt and pepper. Heat oil in large sauté pan over medium heat. Carefully place medallions in pan. Sauté on both sides until medium rare, a few minutes on each side. Set aside and keep warm. Prepare ragout by heating bacon over medium heat until cooked. Add leeks and carrots and cook until soft. Add shallots, garlic, white wine, thyme sprig, bay leaf, and lime juice. Add lentils and chicken stock and reduce heat until lentils are cooked, about 40 minutes. Remove bay leaf and thyme sprig. Place ragout in center of warm dinner plate. Top with two venison medallions. Serve with cherry sauce. Serves 4.

Cherry Sauce

2 shallots, minced
1 quart venison stock
2 shallots, minced
1 ounce crème de cassis
1 tablespoon fresh tarragon,
  chopped

cracked black pepper
salt
¼ pound sun-dried cherries,
  soaked in water overnight

Place venison stock on medium heat and simmer until reduced to ¼ volume. Sauté minced shallots in crème de cassis, add venison stock and tarragon, and simmer until naturally thickened. Adjust seasoning with cracked black pepper and salt. Drain cherries and stir into sauce, cooking until thoroughly heated. Divide sauce into four equal portions and serve hot with venison medallions and lentil ragout. Serves 4.

Casey Moore's Oyster House
At Ninth & Ash

850 South Ash Avenue
TEMPE

*C*asey Moore's Oyster House at Ninth & Ash, located on a quiet corner a few blocks from downtown Tempe and the campus of Arizona State University, offers delighted diners a variety of traditional dishes accompanied, some say, by a cast of ghostly characters. There are many who contend that this com-

11:00 A.M. until 10:30 P.M.
Daily

For reservations
call (602) 968-9935

fortable restaurant is haunted by two elderly ghosts, yet it is agreed that the spirits are friendly. They reportedly can be seen dancing in an upstairs dining room. Theories regarding their identity abound, but the most logical explanation is that the romantic duo is none other than William and Mary Moeur, the couple that built the house in 1910.

Who can blame the Moeurs if they prefer to remain in their former residence, which features distinctive corner bricks, a hipped copper roof, and dormer windows. The home's stately appearance was probably well-suited for Mr. Moeur, a prominent businessman, local politician, justice of the peace, and Arizona's first state land commissioner. With such an illustrious first resident, it stands to reason that the structure is listed in his name on the National Register of Historic Places. William and Mary Moeur eventually died in their cherished home, but their names, and perhaps their spirits, live on.

During the 1930s, the structure became a boarding house—some claim it was actually a house of ill repute—and was later used as a fraternity house. It was converted into a restaurant in the 1980s and, in 1986, was given the name Casey Moore's Oyster House in honor of one of the owner's relatives, a boarding-house operator in Ireland. Recent renovation and expansion projects have resulted in an additional four-hundred-square-foot dining room, an outdoor patio, and an enlarged bar at the restaurant.

When I arrived at Casey Moore's, my table was waiting on the cozy, glass-enclosed side porch. The expanse of windows on the porch provided a view of the surrounding streets in the restaurant's quiet, residential neighborhood, one of the reasons for this restaurant's homey appeal. Dainty flowered wallpaper, stained-glass windows, and delicate lace curtains create a Victorian mood throughout the two levels of dining and make a pleasant backdrop for a memorable meal.

The menu features old photographs of the historic structure along with a sizeable selection of traditional dishes. The appetizer section is lengthy, but the name "Casey Moore's Oyster House" says it all for me. I went with the Oysters Rockefeller, the restaurant's trademark dish. The steaming spinach-topped oysters hidden under a blanket of cheese and bacon were outstanding, so when the chef suggested that I try another house specialty, I didn't argue. Presto, another winner appeared, this time the perfectly grilled Swordfish with Roasted Pepper Butter. Too full for dessert but reluctant to leave, I sipped an Irish Coffee and kept my eyes peeled for one of the resident ghosts. I didn't spot the Moeurs dancing through the dining room, but perhaps I will during my next visit.

Casey Moore's Oyster House at Ninth & Ash's Oysters Rockefeller

1 pint heavy whipping cream
2 bay leaves
½ teaspoon fresh garlic, minced
1 teaspoon chicken stock or base
a pinch of white pepper
¹/₃ pound (approximately 1½ sticks) butter
1 cup flour
¹/₂ cup Parmesan cheese, grated

¾ cup Swiss cheese, grated
½ pound spinach, cooked and drained
1 small white onion, diced
2 tablespoons (1 ounce) bacon grease
¼ cup (2 ounces) anisette
24 fresh oysters in half shell
½ cup bacon bits

In medium saucepan, combine whipping cream, bay leaves, garlic, chicken stock, and pepper. Cook over low heat, stirring occasionally. In separate small saucepan, prepare roux by melting butter. Whisk in flour, a little at a time, until mixture is smooth and thick. Add roux, Parmesan cheese, and Swiss cheese to cream mixture and stir until well blended. In separate saucepan, sauté spinach and onion in bacon grease. Add anisette and reduce to half. Arrange shucked oysters in single layer in large flat baking dish. Top oysters with a dollop of spinach mixture and top spinach mixture with cream sauce. Sprinkle bacon bits over the oysters. Bake in 450-degree oven for 20 minutes. Makes appetizers for 6 to 8.

Casey Moore's Oyster House at Ninth & Ash's Swordfish with Roasted Pepper Butter

1 red bell pepper
½ pound (2 sticks) butter, softened
1 teaspoon black pepper
a pinch of garlic powder

a dash of salt
½ teaspoon parsley
6 swordfish fillets, 8 ounces each

Heat grill and roast red pepper over hot coals until skin is charred and can be removed easily. Peel and finely dice red pepper and set aside. In small bowl, whip butter and add red pepper, black pepper, garlic powder, salt, and parsley. Stir until well blended. Grill swordfish until done, approximately 5 to 7 minutes on each side. Top each fillet with equal portion of pepper butter before serving. Serves 6.

Casey Moore's Oyster House at Ninth & Ash's Irish Coffee

½ teaspoon vanilla
½ teaspoon almond extract
½ cup whipped cream
½ cup hot coffee

1 ounce Irish whiskey
1 cube of sugar
crème de menthe for garnish

In small bowl, gently fold vanilla and almond extract into whipped cream. Pour hot coffee into large mug. Add whiskey and sugar cube and stir until cube is dissolved. Top mug with whipped cream and dribble with crème de menthe. Serves 1.

P. Faires

House of Tricks

114 East Seventh Street
TEMPE

A restaurant with a name like House of Tricks is sure to attract guests looking for a magical dining experience. The fact that the restaurant is named after its owners, Robert and Robin Trick, doesn't mean that there's no magic at this appealing little cottage. The Tricks do their conjuring in the kitchen, and they are winning rave reviews for their culinary wizardry. The restaurant's imaginative dishes have enabled this talented couple to transform a tiny bungalow, with more seating outdoors than in, into one of Tempe's trendiest eateries.

Lunch
11:00 A.M. until 4:00 P.M.
Monday through Friday

Dinner
4:00 P.M. until 9:00 P.M.
Tuesday through Friday

5:00 P.M. until 9:00 P.M.
Saturday

For reservations
(highly recommended)
call (602) 968-1114

The petite stucco structure that houses the restaurant was built in 1920 as a guest and rental cottage for the house next door. Prior to its conversion into a restaurant in 1987, the cottage was used as a blueprint shop and once provided a convenient residence for the secretary to Grady Gammage, Arizona State University's president from 1933 to 1959. During his lengthy tenure, the illustrious Gammage was responsible for much of the university's expansion. The stunning, circular Gammage Auditorium for the Arts, designed by Frank Lloyd Wright, was erected in his memory and is now a Tempe landmark. The restaurant's proximity to the campus, Gammage Auditorium, and Sun Devil Stadium makes it a favorite with performing arts patrons, sports fans, faculty members, and students with educated palates.

There are House of Tricks fans who claim the best place to dine is outside on the patio, under a canopy of flowering vines. Even on cool evenings, a central fireplace on the patio permits alfresco dining. Others swear the best seats are indoors, near the rugged stone fireplace and antique style furnishings or at one of the tables on the enclosed porch. Wherever you end up sitting will be fine because it's the food and the mood that matters most at this restaurant.

The menu appears on a single sheet and changes often. It offers an interesting selection of appetizers, soups, salads, and entrées reflecting the combined flavors of the Southwest and the Mediterranean. And what combinations they are! Huge Portabello Mushrooms with Cilantro Pesto, Ginger Beef in Filo Pastry served with eggplant and hummus, Swordfish and Orzo with Avocado Salsa, and Peppered Pork with Raisins and Couscous are a sample of the wonderful dishes that await the diner. Let me tell you, with temptations like these, decision-making can be an ordeal. The stuffed portabello mushrooms and a glass of chilled Lindeman's 1993 Australian Chardonnay won my vote, then my enthusiasm. My husband, Jon, murmured similar praises between bites of his Stuffed Eggplant Lasagne. Thanks to the chef's recipes, we can recreate the magic in our own kitchen.

The well-trained wait staff, neatly dressed in black and white, adds the proper polish to the restaurant's sophisticated dishes, which arrive perfectly prepared and artistically embellished.

House Of Tricks'
Portabello Mushrooms with Cilantro Pesto

4 large Portabello mushrooms
2 tablespoons olive oil
¾ cup cilantro pesto
 (recipe follows)
½ cup tomato, diced

½ cup mild goat cheese or
 feta cheese
2 tablespoons balsamic
 vinegar
fresh cilantro for garnish

Preheat oven to 350 degrees. Break stems from mushrooms and gently brush off any debris from mushroom caps. Brush olive oil on both sides of mushroom caps, and arrange bottom-side-up on baking sheet to soften and shrink mushrooms. Bake for 20 minutes. Prepare cilantro pesto (see recipe on following page) while mushrooms are baking. Remove mushrooms from oven and set aside until cool enough to handle. Spread pesto evenly over mushrooms and top with diced tomatoes and crumbled goat cheese or feta cheese. Broil in preheated oven for 5 minutes until mushrooms are bubbly and lightly browned. Sprinkle with balsamic vinegar and garnish with cilantro leaves. Serves 4.

Cilantro Pesto

½ cup cilantro leaves
6 tablespoons olive oil
1 tablespoon balsamic vinegar
2 teaspoons lemon juice
3 tablespoons pine nuts

2 cloves garlic, sliced
2 tablespoons Parmesan
   cheese, grated
¼ teaspoon fresh ground pepper
¼ teaspoon salt

In food processor or blender container, combine cilantro leaves, olive oil, balsamic vinegar, lemon juice, pine nuts, and garlic. Blend until well mixed. Stir in Parmesan cheese and season with salt and pepper. If pesto is too thick, thin with a few drops of olive oil. Makes approximately ¾ cup.

House Of Tricks' Stuffed Eggplant Lasagne

4 small round eggplants
1½ pounds ricotta cheese
½ cup Parmesan cheese, grated
2 eggs
½ cup scallions, sliced thin
½ cup sun-dried tomatoes,
   finely chopped

fresh ground pepper
½ teaspoon salt
4 cups rich marinara sauce
4 large lasagne noodles,
   boiled and drained
8 ounces mild goat cheese

Preheat oven to 400 degrees. Cut a horizontal slice across the top of each eggplant. Remove "cap" and hollow out the insides by scraping and cutting with a spoon, leaving ½ inch to 1 inch of flesh on the sides and bottom of eggplant. Bake eggplant shells in oven for 40 minutes. While eggplants are baking, mix ricotta cheese, Parmesan cheese, eggs, scallions, and sun-dried tomatoes. Add salt and pepper to taste. Pour a small amount of marinara sauce in bottom of eggplant and spoon a little of the ricotta mixture over the sauce. Tear noodles in half and lay half of one noodle over the cheese. Crumble half of the goat cheese over top. Repeat with another layer of sauce, ricotta mixture, noodle, and remaining goat cheese. Add final topping of sauce. Bake stuffed eggplants for 35 to 45 minutes in 350-degree oven. Before serving, crumble any remaining cheese over top and serve with the remaining marinara sauce. Serves 4.

Macayo's Depot Cantina

300 South Ash Avenue
TEMPE

11:00 A.M. until 11:00 P.M.
Sunday through Thursday

11:00 A.M. until Midnight
Friday and Saturday

For reservations
call (602) 966-6677

*W*hen the first locomotive chugged into the train depot in Tempe back in 1887, the whole town came out to cheer. The jubilant citizens, no longer isolated from the outside world, recognized the event was a cause for celebration. The original train depot in Tempe is now gone, but the revelry continues at the present Tempe train station, the home of the award-winning Macayo's Depot Cantina.

The train depot, the town's third, was built in 1924 and became part of the Southern Pacific main line in 1925. Constructed of brick, it replaced a wooden depot that was destroyed by fire. In 1987, the old structure was expanded, renovated, and converted into a Mexican-themed restaurant and bar while still functioning as Tempe's train station.

This delightful hacienda-style restaurant offers the best antidote for depression this side of the border, and the fun starts as soon as you arrive. Turquoise wrought-iron gates flanked by old wooden wagon wheels open onto a spacious walled patio that features tables, a mosaic-tiled fountain, a fireplace, and, if you time it right, a strolling mariachi band. Granted, this is an inviting scene, but first-time visitors should resist the urge to grab the first available table on the patio and continue on to the restaurant's interior.

Proceed to the front door and prepare yourself for the fiesta inside. Mechanical figures bob and sway from overhead ledges, T-shirts hang from clotheslines, hubcaps line the walls, and ceiling fans rotate with blades made from badminton rackets. The bar at the right of the entrance is located in the oldest part of the building and is definitely the place to be when a train passes the restaurant. To celebrate this event, robots dance, whistles blow, and bells ring. The carnival continues in the large dining room, which features an enormous chandelier constructed from 999 Mexican beer bottles. Bright colors are splashed everywhere—on the floors, on the walls, and even on the menu, which offers enough tempting selections to please any Mexican-food fan. There are also plenty of heart-healthy dishes for fat and cholesterol counters.

I arrived with my family on a sunny Sunday in January, just in time for brunch. This weekend event was a fine opportunity to sample a wide variety of the restaurant's Mexican specialties. From a well-stocked buffet, we created our own combination plates piled high with enchiladas, tostadas, chimichangas, taquitos, and rellenos. A return trip to the buffet soon followed our initial visit, this time for a sampling of the restaurant's delicious desserts. Our unanimous favorites were the crusty Fried Ice Cream topped with honey and whipped cream and the rich Double Fudge Layered Cake.

Can you blame us for not wanting to leave our table on the sunny patio, with the fountain bubbling and mariachis serenading? Instead, we decided to wait for a train to appear on the tracks running behind and beside the restaurant and the celebration that follows. Alas, no trains appeared. But it didn't matter because a Sunday afternoon at Macayo's Depot Cantina is cause enough for celebration.

Macayo's Depot Cantina's Blue Corn Chicken Enchiladas

1 cup olive oil
1 teaspoon chile tepin, crushed
1 teaspoon oregano
½ teaspoon thyme
1 teaspoon marjoram
1½ teaspoons rosemary
2 garlic cloves, minced
2 chicken breasts,
   7 ounces each

8 blue corn tortillas,
   10-inch size
5 tablespoons onions, diced
5 tablespoons green chilies,
   diced
2 cups Monterey Jack cheese,
   shredded
2 cups green chile sauce
   (recipe follows)

Combine olive oil, chile tepin, oregano, thyme, marjoram, rosemary, and garlic together in bowl. Whisk until well blended. Add chicken and marinate for 2 hours or overnight. Remove chicken from marinade and grill chicken breasts for 5 minutes on each side. When cool enough to handle, pull chicken apart into thin strands. In separate bowl, combine chicken pieces, onions, green chilies, and one cup cheese and mix well. In saucepan, warm green chile sauce. Dip each tortilla into the warm sauce until tortilla is lightly coated with sauce. Place about 2 tablespoons of chicken mixture across the center of each tortilla. Loosely roll up filled tortillas and set them, side by side, in ovenproof dish. Cover enchiladas with remaining sauce and sprinkle with remaining cheese. Put dish into 350-degree oven and bake until enchiladas are heated through, no more than 15 minutes. Serve immediately. Makes 8 enchiladas or 4 servings.

Green Chile Sauce

2 tablespoons vegetable oil
1 cup onions, chopped
4 tablespoons all-purpose flour
2 cups mild green chilies,
　chopped

2 cups chicken broth
½ teaspoon garlic powder
1½ teaspoons salt

Heat oil in medium saucepan over medium heat until hot. Add onions and sauté until tender. Add flour and cook, stirring constantly, until a brown roux is formed. Add chilies, chicken broth, garlic powder, and salt and stir until well blended. Simmer sauce for 20 minutes. Makes 4 cups.

Mill Landing Restaurant

398 South Mill Avenue
TEMPE

Valley of the Sun residents have been known to brag long and hard about the area's endless supply of sun-filled days. It's doubtful, however, that the boasters would actually risk losing money on the claim. But back in the first part of the century, the Casa Loma Hotel did that very thing. Their policy of not charging guests for days when there was no sunshine must surely have tickled its guests and occasionally drained the hotel's coffers.

11:00 A.M. until 10:00 P.M.
Monday through Thursday

11:00 A.M. until 11:00 P.M.
Friday and Saturday

10:00 A.M. until 10:00 P.M.
Sunday

For reservations
(advised)
call (602) 966-1700

The hotel would not have lost money on the day I arrived at the Mill Landing Restaurant, which is situated on the first floor of the old Casa Loma Hotel building. The sun was shining brightly on the attractive pink stucco structure, one of the oldest and most colorful buildings in downtown Tempe's Old Town area. Built in 1899, the three-story building replaced a wooden structure built in 1888 which was later destroyed by fire. Originally named the Atwood Hotel, the new building became the Hotel Casa Loma in 1901 and quickly rose to fame as Tempe's grandest hotel. The hotel also served as a hub for the town's social and commercial life. Among the famous who stayed at the celebrated hotel were President William McKinley and Buffalo Bill Cody.

In 1927, a remodeling project transformed the building's brick facade into the Spanish-colonial-style exterior that is still seen today. After serving for a half-century as Tempe's finest hotel, the structure was converted into apartments. Another forty years passed before a restaurant returned to the old building, continuing the grand tradition of the hotel.

There are those who will tell you that the best place to sit at Mill Landing Restaurant is indoors under the high ceilings where plants tumble from hanging pots. Granted, the dining rooms are lovely with their original exposed brick walls and the soft floral fabrics on the chairs and booths. But I wanted alfresco dining in the warm December sunshine.

From my table under a bright-green umbrella on the front patio, I watched passersby strolling along a sidewalk lined with fruit-laden orange trees. The fresh air seemed to stimulate my appetite, which intensified as I read the menu. Seafood and steak dishes take top billing here, but there are enough interesting choices to please even the pickiest diner. I ordered a steaming bowl of Clam Chowder, an award-winning item at this restaurant. My wise server suggested a glass of chilled Sauvignon Blanc as an accompaniment to my entrée selection, Salmon Oscar, and I heartily agreed. All the choices proved to be excellent and were quickly devoured. I made a note to return in the evening, when musicians entertain on the patio to the delight of diners and passersby.

Mill Landing Restaurant's Clam Chowder

2 cups medium potatoes,
    peeled and diced
4 strips bacon
4 tablespoons margarine
¾ cup flour
¼ cup celery, diced
¼ cup onion, diced

1 quart water
4 small cans chopped clams
    with juice
¼ teaspoon white pepper
½ teaspoon thyme
1 cup heavy cream
½ cup (1 stick) butter

Blanch potatoes in boiling water until barely tender, approximately 5 minutes. Rinse under cold water, drain, and set aside. Sauté the bacon in 4-quart saucepan over medium heat until crisp. Remove bacon from pan, dice, and set aside. Add 2 tablespoons margarine to bacon drippings in pan. Prepare roux by whisking in flour and mixing well over low heat for 3 to 4 minutes until thick. Remove roux from pot and set aside. Add remaining 2 tablespoons margarine to pot and sauté celery and onions over low heat until vegetables are soft. Return roux to pot. Add water and juice from canned clams. Raise heat to high and cook for 6 to 8 minutes or until mixture thickens, stirring frequently. Add clams, bacon, potatoes, white pepper, thyme, and cream. Simmer for 5 minutes. Serve pat of butter atop each serving. Makes 2 quarts.

Mill Landing Restaurant's Crab-Stuffed Mushroom Caps

1 tablespoon olive oil
¼ cup bell pepper,
  finely chopped
¼ cup celery, finely chopped
¼ cup onion, finely chopped
1 cup seasoned bread crumbs
¼ cup fresh parsley, chopped
1 cup snow crabmeat

a dash of salt and pepper
½ teaspoon thyme
¼ cup (½ stick)
  margarine
¼ cup (½ stick) butter
24 large mushrooms,
  stems removed
6 slices havarti cheese

In skillet, heat olive oil and sauté bell peppers, celery, and onions until transparent. Remove from heat and let cool. In medium-sized mixing bowl, combine sautéed vegetables, bread crumbs, parsley, and crabmeat, blending well. Season with salt, pepper, and thyme. Set aside. Melt margarine and butter in pan and sauté mushroom caps for 8 to 10 minutes. Drain and let cool. Fill mushroom caps with stuffing and place in shallow baking dish. Divide each cheese slice into quarters and add one piece to the top of each mushroom cap. Bake at 400 degrees until cheese is thoroughly melted. Serve hot. Makes 24 appetizers.

Monti's La Casa Vieja

3 West First Street
TEMPE

$\mathscr{M}$onti's La Casa Vieja Restaurant is located in the oldest remaining building in the Salt River Valley and is considered to be the most significant historic resource in Tempe. It was built in 1871, a year after an ambitious entrepreneur by the name of Charles Trumbull Hayden climbed a butte overlooking the Salt River Valley and first laid eyes on the wide river and the miles of irrigation canals built by the ancient Hohokam Indians. Hayden envisioned a prosperous future in what he saw. He selected a spot along the Salt River's banks where he launched a ferry service and built a home. He then constructed a blacksmith shop and flour mill. Eventually, a tiny settlement known as Hayden's Ferry sprung up at the site. By the time Hayden's Ferry was renamed Tempe in 1879, the industrious Charles Hayden, "the Father of Tempe," had carved his name into Arizona's history.

11:00 A.M. until 11:00 P.M.
Sunday through Thursday

11:00 A.M. until Midnight
Friday and Saturday

For information
and reservations
call (602) 967-7594

Today, many of the structures built by Charles Hayden still stand. His century-old flour mill remains the oldest continuously operated business in Arizona, and his former home has been expanded into a popular restaurant. The original adobe walls and willow ceiling poles are still seen in the residence, which is also the birthplace of Carl Hayden, Arizona's longest serving United States senator. The Spanish-style hacienda, built around a large outdoor patio, played many roles during the city's early history. A plaque near the entrance describes how the house served as a rallying place for Tempe suffragettes led by Charles Hayden's wife, Sallie. Later, the house became the Hayden Hotel.

In 1924, new owners remodeled the historic building and converted it into a restaurant. Today, it is one of Arizona's oldest eating establishments. The restaurant's name, La Casa Vieja, means "the old house" in Spanish. Once you set foot inside the front door you'll agree that the name fits. Throughout the years, additions have been made to this sprawling restaurant, but the preservation-minded Monti family, who purchased the building in 1956, have taken pains to preserve the structure's original features and its history. The uneven river-rock floors in the entrance may present a challenge to those in anything but flat-heeled shoes, but they are authentic, as are the old photographs and blueprints located in the lounge near the entrance.

Monti's La Casa Vieja features twelve dining rooms, each with a different decor and mood. My favorite is the spacious former courtyard. Although it was enclosed many years ago, the room still has an open-air feeling, due in part to the colorful, century-old fountain with mosaic tiles and the rough stone fireplace. It seemed like a perfect room to enjoy one of the juicy steaks that this restaurant has built a reputation on.

The menu features an ample selection of traditional fare, including seafood dishes and a few poultry selections. There is even a spaghetti plate made from an old Monti-family recipe. But the main focus at Monti's La Casa Vieja is on choice cuts of beef offered at reasonable prices.

One of the restaurant's signature items is the rosemary-flavored Roman Bread, made from another Monti-family recipe brought from Rome over seventy years ago. It proved a worthy accompaniment for my dinner salad, which arrived covered with a mound of thick, chunky Roquefort Dressing. My filet mignon arrived from the broiler just as I had hoped—hot, juicy, deep pink in the center, and lightly charred on the outside. Since I proceeded to finish everything on my plate, I had no room for dessert. However, I did make a note to return for a slice of the White Chocolate Raspberry Cheesecake that was winning raves at the next table.

Monti's La Casa Vieja's Roman Bread

1½ cups lukewarm water　　*2 teaspoons salt*
1 tablespoon granulated sugar　*½ cup onion, finely chopped*
1 cake (0.6 ounce) yeast　　*½ cup dried rosemary*
4 cups all-purpose flour

Pour water into large mixing bowl. Add sugar and yeast, stirring until yeast is dissolved. Mix in flour, 1½ teaspoons salt, and onion and knead until mixture becomes a smooth dough. Place dough in an oiled bowl and let rise until double in size. Punch dough down and flatten on an oiled cookie sheet to about 1-inch thick. Sprinkle with dried rosemary and additional ½ teaspoon salt. Bake at 400 degrees for 20 to 25 minutes. Serve hot. Serves 6 to 8.

Monti's La Casa Vieja's Spaghetti and Meat Sauce

2 tablespoons olive oil
2 pounds ground beef
¹/₃ cup sweet dried basil
1 small garlic clove, minced
½ cup bell pepper, chopped
½ cup onion, chopped
½ cup celery, chopped
½ cup carrots, chopped

1 can (16 ounces)
   tomato purée
1 can (16 ounces)
   whole tomatoes
¼ pound salt pork, diced
salt and pepper to taste
1 pound spaghetti,
   cooked and drained

Heat olive oil over medium to high heat in large heavy skillet or saucepan. Add ground beef and cook until meat is brown. Drain beef well, return to skillet, and stir in remaining ingredients. Simmer for 2 to 3 hours, stirring occasionally, until sauce has thickened and flavors are well blended. Prepare spaghetti according to package directions and drain well. Pour sauce over pasta, coating well. Serves 4 to 6.

Monti's La Casa Vieja's Roquefort Dressing

1 cup commercial sour cream
   with chives
1 cup sour cream

1 tablespoon lemon juice
¾ cup Roquefort cheese

In medium bowl, mix together sour creams and lemon juice using a wooden spoon. Break cheese into small pieces by hand and fold into sour cream mixture. Chill well before serving. Yields approximately 2½ cups.

D. Faires

The Paradise Bar And Grill

401 South Mill Avenue
TEMPE

In 1900, when R.G. Andre was searching for a location for his saddle-and-harness shop, Tempe's main thoroughfare was a wide, dusty road known as Mill Avenue. It stands to reason that Mr. Andre would choose this busy road as a location for the handsome brick structure that would house his shop.

Wagons no longer scatter dust along Mill Avenue, but the Andre Building, which now houses the Paradise Bar and Grill, has retained its prominent place in the heart of busy downtown Tempe. Considered one of the best-preserved territorial commercial buildings in the city, the historic structure has accommodated a variety of establishments throughout its history. A funeral parlor, meat market, pool hall, Wells Fargo Express Company office, and a post office have all taken advantage of the building's prime commercial location. In 1979, the Andre Building was placed on the National Register of Historic Places, and three years later, it became a restaurant.

11:00 A.M. until 10:30 P.M.
Sunday through Thursday

11:00 A.M. until 11:30 P.M.
Friday and Saturday

Dinner Entrées
5:00 P.M. until closing
Daily

For reservations
(for parties of eight or more)
call (602) 829-0606

Tempe's old downtown commercial area is now referred to as "Old Town." It is an active place, popular with shoppers and college students from nearby Arizona State University who like to mill around the area's shaded sidewalks and visit the many shops, restaurants, and coffee houses. The Paradise Bar and Grill is a particular favorite of football fans who crowd into the restaurant before and after heading to nearby Sun Devil Stadium to cheer for the Arizona State Sun Devils or the Phoenix Cardinals. Even when there isn't a football game, the spacious bar and lounge area is usually packed. Another popular location in this restaurant is the back patio, a favorite spot for people-watchers. However, I bypassed both of these areas for a cozy booth in the restaurant's attractive dining room located to the right of the entrance.

The restaurant's current owner has taken care to preserve many of the building's original features. The storefront and the brick walls appear much as they did almost a century ago, and the reproduced pressed-metal ceiling matches the original. However, the interior has a casual, contemporary flavor with plenty of shiny brass, greenery, and servers scurrying about in khaki pants and polo shirts.

The food at this eatery is as casually appealing as the decor. Snacking is a favorite pastime here, and the menu offers an interesting selection of appetizers and lighter-fare items, along with some sophisticated entrées. I noticed a plateful of onion rings and cheese-topped potato skins being devoured at a nearby booth, while a group at another table vigorously attacked mounds of shrimp wontons and chicken tenders. My mouth was beginning to water, so my order of Lahvosh, an Armenian cracker topped with cheese, ham, bacon, and assorted vegetables, couldn't have arrived at a better time. This tasty appetizer was gobbled up in no time, making the wait for my dinner entrée tolerable. The short wait was worth it, though, since the Lemon Pepper Chicken with Artichoke Hearts was delicious. This dish was definitely worth an effort to get the recipe, and thanks to the obliging chef, it is now possible for us to experience a bit of "Paradise" in our own kitchens.

The Paradise Bar and Grill's Lahvosh

1 round lahvosh cracker bread
    (15 inches)
6 slices (1 ounce)
    havarti cheese
¼ cup tomatoes, diced
¼ cup mushrooms,
    sliced and cooked
2 tablespoons bacon,
    diced, cooked, and drained

2 tablespoons ham,
    diced and cooked
¼ cup green pepper, chopped
4 artichoke hearts, quartered
¼ cup green onions, diced
¼ cup pineapple chunks,

Place cracker bread on pizza pan, seeded side up. Lay cheese slices over bread and top with remaining ingredients. Place in oven and bake at 375 degrees until cheese is completely melted, about 4 to 5 minutes. Slice into serving pieces. Makes 4 appetizer servings.

The Paradise Bar and Grill's Five-Minute Caesar Salad

3 cups whole mayonnaise
1 tablespoons red wine vinegar
1½ tablespoons fresh lemon juice
1 clove garlic, minced
½ teaspoon black pepper,
  coarsely grated
2 tablespoons Dijon mustard

6 tablespoons Parmesan
  cheese, grated
1½ teaspoons anchovy paste
2 bunches romaine lettuce,
  chopped
¼ head red cabbage, chopped
1 box seasoned croutons

In mixing bowl, combine mayonnaise, vinegar, lemon juice, garlic, pepper, mustard, Parmesan cheese, and anchovy paste and mix well.

Place lettuce and cabbage into large salad bowl, pour dressing over top, and toss well, until lettuce is covered. Top each serving with croutons and additional Parmesan cheese. Makes about 3½ cups dressing. Serves 4 to 6.

The Paradise Bar and Grill's Lemon Pepper Chicken with Artichoke Hearts

4 chicken breasts
  (5 to 6 ounces each),
  boneless and skinless
4 tablespoons lemon pepper
  seasoning

2 tablespoons olive oil
1 can (14 ounces)
  artichoke hearts

Sprinkle chicken breasts on both sides with lemon pepper seasoning and place in baking dish. Broil in oven until done, approximately 5 to 7 minutes on each side. While chicken is broiling, heat olive oil in saucepan and sauté artichokes until hot. To serve, place chicken on plate and top with artichoke hearts. Serves 4.

The Landmark Restaurant

809 West Main Street
MESA

rue to its name, the Landmark Restaurant is located in one of the most historically significant structures in Mesa, the third largest city in Arizona. Erected in 1908, the gable-roofed, red-brick building still resembles a Mormon church—its first role. In its original setting, the church was situated beside a peaceful canal and surrounded by towering cottonwood trees. However, the building's present location at the corner of a busy intersection bears no resemblance to that earlier setting.

Lunch
11:30 A.M. until 2:00 P.M.
Monday through Friday

Dinner
4:00 P.M. until 9:00 P.M.
Monday through Saturday

Noon until 7:00 P.M.
Sunday

No reservations
For information
call (602) 962-4652

During its fifty years of operation, the church and its membership grew along with the surrounding city. An expansion project in 1939 enlarged the church to its present size, but by the late 1950s, the congregation found it necessary to relocate to a larger facility. However, the old church building still had plenty of life in it. In 1963, it became the original campus of Mesa Community College. A decade later, the church was transformed into a restaurant.

In a city where Mexican cafes and western steakhouses are the norm, the Landmark Restaurant has earned a reputation for serving tasty, home-style dishes with a midwestern flavor. The restaurant is also known for serving up a healthy dose of Arizona history. Downstairs in the former Sunday-school area, an impressive collection of historical photos lines the walls of the halls, overflow dining rooms, and the parlor-sized lounge. Upstairs in the main dining room, the mood is proper Victorian. Dainty lace curtains and rose-patterned wallpaper combine with antique reproductions to lend an air of formality to the high-ceilinged room.

The Salad Room is one of the most popular features of this appealing restaurant, and one that you will not want to miss. If you can imagine an entire room devoted to salad fixings, then you'll believe it when I say the Salad Room contains everything from capers to pickled herring, thick creamy homemade soups to nuts, and fresh-baked cookies for dessert. How I managed to maneuver back to my table in the main dining room without spilling a morsel from my overloaded plate remains a mystery.

Traditional midwestern dishes are the pride of the Landmark's kitchen and are best described as meals that would have made your grandmother swoon. As I read the menu that included listings for Chicken Pot Pie, Sautéed Liver with Onions and Bacon, Chicken-Fried Steak, and Roast Turkey with Sage Stuffing and Giblet Gravy, I thought about grandma and ordered one of her old favorites, Pot Roast and Gravy. It was so tender and stringy I could cut it with a fork, just like hers.

A plain cup of decaffeinated coffee was all I had in mind for dessert until I spotted the Bread Pudding. Nostalgia struck me again as I savored the warm moist square of cinnamon-and-nut-filled bread pudding topped with warm lemon sauce. I cleaned my plate, knowing grandma would have been pleased.

Landmark Restaurant's Bread Pudding

3 large eggs
1¼ cups sugar
1½ teaspoons vanilla
½ teaspoon nutmeg
1½ teaspoons cinnamon
½ cup melted butter

2 cups whole milk
½ cup raisins
½ cup pecans, coarsely
   chopped
5 cups stale bread pieces,
   packed

In large bowl, beat eggs with mixer approximately 3 minutes until frothy. Add sugar, vanilla, nutmeg, cinnamon, and melted butter. Whip until well blended. Add milk, mixing well. Stir in raisins and pecans. Place bread pieces into bottom of well-greased 8-inch or 9-inch baking pan or casserole dish. Pour egg-milk mixture over bread, tossing lightly until bread is well soaked. Let stand for 45 minutes. Cover pan and bake for 1 hour at 350 degrees. Remove cover and continue to bake until browned, approximately 5 minutes. Serve topped with whipped cream and/or commercial chocolate, caramel, or lemon sauce. Serves 4 generously.

½ cup salad oil
1 teaspoon thyme
1 teaspoon black pepper
1 clove garlic, crushed
5 pounds chuck roast
2 cups tomato juice

2 quarts beef stock, broth,
  or bouillon
2 carrots, peeled and diced
2 onions, diced
1 bay leaf

In small bowl combine salad oil, thyme, pepper, and crushed garlic. Mix well. Rub mixture into chuck roast and place in heavy baking pan or casserole dish. Pour tomato juice over meat. Bake for 20 minutes at 400 degrees until lightly browned. Add the beef stock, carrots, onion, and bay leaf. Cover pot tightly and bake 3 hours or until beef is very tender. Check periodically to ensure that liquid does not evaporate. If necessary, add water to bring liquid to original level. Serves 8 to 10.

Brown Gravy

½ cup (1 stick) butter
½ cup flour
2 to 3 cups broth
  from pot roast

salt and pepper to taste

Heat butter in medium saucepan over medium heat until very hot. Mix flour into butter, whisking until smooth. Cook for 3 minutes, stirring constantly. In another pan, bring broth to a boil. Reduce heat and slowly stir flour and butter mixture into broth with wire whip or whisk, blending until smooth. If sauce becomes too thick, add more broth. Add salt and pepper and lightly simmer for 15 minutes. Serve over tender pot roast slices.

1912

Sheraton San Marcos Resort • One San Marcos Place
CHANDLER

The year 1912 was a significant one in the Grand Canyon State's history. It was the year Arizona achieved statehood, and the year ground was broken for the state's first public resort, the elegant San Marcos Hotel in Chandler. It stands to reason that a restaurant located in the San Marcos, considered to be the prototype of southwestern resorts, would be named after such an important year.

4:30 P.M. until 10:00 P.M.
Daily

For reservations
(recommended)
call (602) 963-6655

The San Marcos, which is listed on the National Register of Historic Places, was the brainchild of wealthy landowner A.J. Chandler, the first Veterinary Surgeon for the Arizona Territory and founder of the city which bears his name. The enterprising doctor hired the West's best architects and craftsmen to design and build the handsome structure. The San Marcos opened in 1913 and soon became known as one of the nation's finest resorts. The glamorous hotel catered to the rich and famous, offering a hundred-acre golf course, retail shops, fine dining, and a constant flow of social activities. News of the luxurious desert retreat quickly spread to Hollywood, and the Chandler resort became a favorite playground for screen stars like Erroll Flynn, Joan Crawford, Fred Astaire, and Gloria Swanson.

Throughout its dazzling history, the legendary resort underwent a series of expansions and renovations. Eventually, it suffered a period of neglect. However, in 1986, a multi-million dollar expansion-and-renovation project was launched by the resort's current owners who have returned the San Marcos to its legendary splendor. Perhaps the most romantic items to resurface during restoration are the pergolas, the vine-covered passageways that once surrounded the entire structure. One of these flower-studded pergolas stretches above the entrance to the 1912 restaurant, located in the resort's oldest building.

The 1912 is considered the more formal of the resort's side-by-side restaurants, but this designation applies more to the restaurant's dinnertime serving hours than to the decor, which is anything but stuffy. Soft shades of sand, mauve, and turquoise appear throughout the intimate, two-tiered dining room. Comfortable wicker chairs and colorful local artwork add a casual touch, while crisp table linens and servers in black and white add the polish. The cuisine is an interesting blend of classical and southwestern that matches the restaurant's relaxed mood.

The uncomplicated menu does not overwhelm diners with selections. One side lists "American Fare," an assortment of standard appetizers, sandwiches, salads, and four entrées. The adventurous will want to consider the more exciting Mexican- and western-inspired items on the menu's other side. These dishes highlight the talents of the inventive chef, who uses his culinary prowess to turn out tantalizing appetizers like Smoked Duck Tacos and Black Bean Pizza, and entrées like Jalapeno-Smoked Shrimp, Anaheim Chili–Stuffed Chicken Breast with Chile Crepes, and Pork Tenderloin stuffed with Grilled Fruit and Cheese. The restaurant's listing of fine wines and selection of tempting desserts appear on menu-sized clay tiles which are standard fixtures on each table.

1912's Santa Fe Roll

1 12-inch flour tortilla
6 tablespoons black beans,
  puréed
1 roasted red bell pepper
2 heaping tablespoons fresh
  spinach, blanched

4 tablespoons Boursin cheese
2 tablespoons Ranchero sauce
  (recipe follows)

Place tortilla flat on a working surface. Spread black bean purée across the bottom quarter of tortilla from side to side. Remove the skin and seeds from the red pepper and cut into 4 sections. Lay pepper sections, side by side, above layer of bean purée. Lay out spinach in same fashion above pepper sections. Spread Boursin cheese on remaining portion of tortilla up to ¼-inch away from edge. Starting at bean end, roll tortilla tightly in jelly-roll or pinwheel fashion. Roll again in clear plastic wrap to protect and hold the shape. Chill before serving. To serve, place 2 tablespoons Ranchero sauce in middle of three serving plates. Using diagonal slices, cut roll into 12 slices. On each plate, place tip of each slice into the sauce and arrange pieces into shape of a star. Serves 3.

Ranchero Sauce

½ large yellow onion, diced
1 medium green pepper, diced
¼ tablespoon fresh garlic,
  minced
2 tablespoons water
2 tablespoons
  Worcestershire sauce
¼ teaspoon Tabasco sauce

1 tablespoon chili powder
½ teaspoon cumin
¼ cup white wine
1 tablespoon white vinegar
½ teaspoon oregano
½ teaspoon coriander
2 cups tomato purée
1 cup tomato paste

Sauté onions, peppers, and garlic with water for about 5 minutes until vegetables are tender. Add Worcestershire, Tabasco, chili powder, cumin, wine, vinegar, oregano, and coriander and sauté for a few minutes. Add tomato purée and tomato paste and cook over low heat for about 1 hour. Drain through fine sieve before serving. Makes about 4 cups.

1912's Bananas Caramel

3 bananas
1½ cups commercial
  caramel sauce

1½ ounces banana liqueur
1 quart vanilla ice cream
1 ounce chopped nuts

Peel and slice bananas. Place in sauté pan and add caramel sauce and banana liqueur. Simmer over low heat for 5 minutes. Remove from heat, set aside, and keep warm. Place 1 scoop ice cream in each of 6 dessert glasses or dishes. Follow with equal amounts of banana mixture. Top each serving with chopped nuts. Serves 6.

Blue Ribbon Cafe

474 North Broad Street
GLOBE

The Blue Ribbon Cafe is known for its good, old-fashioned cooking—the kind of dishes that would win prizes at county fairs and praises at church picnics. But back in the early 1900s, during the mining heyday in the town of Globe, the reputation of the building that houses the Blue Ribbon Cafe could hardly have been considered wholesome.

6:30 A.M. until 9:00 P.M.
Monday through Friday

7:30 A.M. until 9:00 P.M.
Saturday and Sunday

For reservations
or information
call (520) 425-4423

Built between 1898 and 1901, the historic, two-story building originally housed a saloon on the first floor. Located in the town's notorious "red light" district, the popular watering hole attracted area miners, as well as the enterprising and colorful "ladies of the night" who conducted their business with the miners upstairs at the Saint Elmo Hotel.

Today, the building that once housed the infamous saloon and hotel is no longer located in the "wrong" part of town. In 1991, it was converted into a charming, respectable restaurant, and it now enjoys a distinguished address in Globe's historic district. The area's miners still frequent the former watering hole, but these days instead of ordering up an intoxicating brew, they're likely to ask for a "Pasty." This tasty meat-and-potato pie, a specialty at the cafe, is made from a recipe said to have originated in a mining community in Cornwall, England.

The Blue Ribbon Cafe's rather plain exterior disguises the Victorian atmosphere that waits inside in the entrance parlor. High ceilings and ruffled curtains combine with chairs, footstools, and assorted antiques to create an appealing welcome. The dining room, located towards the rear of the building, is cheerful, relaxed, and friendly with wooden tables covered by bright-blue linens.

Home cooking is the specialty at this restaurant. The menu combines breakfast, lunch, and dinner fare and offers many familiar dishes. A big winner with the Sunday breakfast crowd is Old-Fashioned Homemade Biscuits and Sausage Gravy. The daily specials, like Chicken and Dumplings, are favorites with the cafe's regular customers. Luncheon selections are mainly hot and cold sandwiches—

hot roast beef, clubs, French Dip, and burgers. For dieters, there's a grilled skinless chicken breast served with salad, fruit, and vegetables. Dinner entrées run the gambit from lasagne and fried chicken to prime rib and shrimp scampi, all served with soup or salad, vegetables, fresh-baked bread, and potatoes.

Whatever you do, save room for a slice of one of the Blue Ribbon's famous homemade pies, some prepared from the owner's century-old family recipes. You'll be transported back to the fairgrounds or church picnics with the first sweet bite. The hard part is choosing between apple, cherry, chocolate, coconut cream, banana cream, tropical delight, strawberry, and lemon meringue. Because you probably won't be satisfied with just one slice, the kitchen offers whole pies to go.

Blue Ribbon Cafe's Chicken and Dumplings

2 whole chickens
1 teaspoon black pepper
1 tablespoon granulated garlic
3 teaspoons salt
3 cups all-purpose flour

4 tablespoons baking powder
½ cup vegetable shortening
¾ cup milk
¾ cup buttermilk

Place whole chickens, pepper, granulated garlic, and 1½ teaspoons salt in large stock pot. Fill pot half full with water, making sure chickens are completely covered. Bring to boil and cook chickens 1½ to 2 hours until done. Remove chickens from pot and set aside to cool. In large bowl, combine flour, remaining salt, and baking powder. Cut in shortening until mixture is consistency of coarse meal. In another bowl, combine milk and buttermilk. Add to flour mixture, mixing well. Place dough on floured board. Knead gently until dough is slightly firm. Pat dough until about 2-inches thick. Use a 2-inch circular cutter to carve dumplings. Skin and remove cooled chicken from bones. Leave chicken in large pieces and return to broth. Bring broth to boil and add dumplings. Cover pot and boil for 20 minutes. Serves 4 to 6.

Crust

1 cup flour
1/2 teaspoon salt
1/3 cup shortening

2 tablespoons ice water

In bowl, combine flour and salt. Cut in shortening until mixture is consistency of coarse meal. Add ice water, one tablespoon at a time, until mixture stays together when formed into a ball. Roll out on floured board until about 1/8-inch thick. Place in 9-inch pie pan and crimp around edges. Prick crust several times with fork. Bake in 350-degree oven for 10 to 12 minutes. Set aside to cool.

Filling

2 cups evaporated milk
1/2 cup water
2¼ cups sugar
3 tablespoons flour
1/2 teaspoon salt

4 tablespoons cocoa
4 egg yolks, beaten
1 tablespoon butter
1 teaspoon vanilla
4 egg whites

In medium saucepan, combine milk and water. Bring to scalding (not boiling) point. In another bowl, combine 1½ cups sugar, flour, salt, and cocoa. Add egg yolks and mix into a thick batter. Add batter to milk-water mixture, stirring constantly with whisk. Cook over medium heat until thickened. Remove from heat and add butter and vanilla, stirring well to blend. Pour into baked pie shell and allow to cool. Prepare meringue by beating egg whites at high speed in bowl until stiff. Add remaining ¾ cup sugar and beat until peaks form. Top pie with meringue. Bake in 350-degree oven for about 6 to 8 minutes until top is golden brown. Cool and serve. Makes 1 pie.

BeDillon's Cactus Garden Restaurant

800 North Park Avenue
CASA GRANDE

Like many Arizona towns, Casa Grande's roots are tied to the railroad industry. Its location at the end of a Southern Pacific line earned the small community the original name of Terminus. But when work on the railroad came to a halt in 1879, the name no longer suited the small band of residents who dreamed of a thriving future for their town. So they renamed the town Casa Grande, Spanish for "Big House," in honor of the prehistoric, five-story structure built by the Hohokam Indians located nearby.

Lunch
11:00 A.M. until 2:00 P.M.
Monday through Friday

Dinner
5:30 P.M. until 9:30 P.M.
Monday through Thursday

For reservations
(recommended)
call (520) 836-2045

The town burned three times between 1884 and 1914, but each time the persistent residents managed to rebuild. The fact that Casa Grande is now a bustling center of activity instead of a ghost town can be directly traced to the determination of those early citizens armed with their visions of progress.

One pair of early residents who managed to make their dreams come true through determination and leave behind a remarkable historical legacy were Mattie and Jean Vallette. During the construction of their home in 1924, the preservation-minded couple began to collect area artifacts and native plants. Eventually, they amassed enough relics and antiques to fill a twelve-hundred-square-foot museum. They also cultivated a cactus garden containing over a hundred species of native plants and other plant specimens from around the world. Today, the museum and gardens can be seen in their original locations behind the old Vallette home, which was converted into BeDillon's Cactus Garden Restaurant in 1986. The restaurant's owners, Michael and Nancy Jackson, also possess a strong regard for history. They have ensured that the priceless collection of artifacts and cacti will never be sold or disturbed by having eleven deed restrictions placed on the property.

Pink adobe walls enclose the old homestead, which is located on a corner in a quiet residential neighborhood near downtown Casa Grande. The restaurant's five dining rooms have a rustic, romantic charm that may leave you feeling somewhat nostalgic—a result, no doubt, of the old home's antique furnishings, beamed ceilings, and original stone fireplace. My table overlooking the sun-washed patio and garden provided a view of the century-old boojum tree, the pride of the cactus garden. It also gave me an opportunity to enjoy the wonderful aromas of the regional American and Mexican dishes that have earned BeDillon's Cactus Garden Restaurant a strong following.

From a luncheon menu listing an assortment of appetizers, sandwiches, salads, and several daily specials, I chose the Pollo Sandia with Fruit Salsa. This oversized salad piled high in a crisp tortilla shell, features grilled chicken with a chunky, fresh-fruit salsa generously seasoned with fresh cilantro and is served with a honey-mustard dressing on the side. The sweet and tangy concoction was so good, I begged for the recipe. Ditto the yummy Fideo, a tasty little side dish of pasta bits sprinkled with enough jalapeno peppers to give my taste buds a healthy kick. What could I do except cool things down with a slice of Apple Cake topped with whipped cream.

Next time I'll dine under the stars on the spacious patio and order a BeDillon's Tequila Sunrise. This popular drink includes juice from the prickly pear cactus, which provide's the drink's deep-purple color and is said to contain eleven times more vitamin C than orange juice. I will drink it for my health, of course.

BeDillon's Cactus Garden Restaurant's Tequila Sunrise

ice cubes
1 ounce tequila
3 ounces orange juice,
   freshly squeezed

1½ ounces prickly pear
   cactus juice

Pour ice cubes into 9-ounce glass. Add tequila, orange juice, and cactus juice. Stir gently and serve. Serves 1.

BeDillon's Cactus Garden Restaurant's Fideo

1 package (8 ounces)
  coiled vermicelli
¼ cup cooking oil
½ onion, chopped
1 clove garlic
1 mild green chile,
  seeded and chopped

1 tomato, chopped
1½ cups chicken broth
salt to taste
½ cup sour cream
1 small bunch
  cilantro leaves

Crumble pasta into small bits and pieces by pressing a rolling pin over the unopened package of vermicelli. Heat oil over medium heat in a large skillet. Sauté the vermicelli in oil, stirring constantly, until golden brown. Push to one side of pan and add onion, garlic, and chile. Cook until onion is soft. Add tomato and stir to mix vermicelli with chile/tomato mixture. Add chicken broth and bring to boil. Reduce heat, cover, and simmer until the liquid has been absorbed, about 15 to 20 minutes. Add salt if needed. Serve garnished with a dollop of sour cream and fresh cilantro leaves. Serves 4 to 6.

BeDillon's Cactus Garden Restaurant's Pollo Sandia with Fruit Salsa

4 plum tomatoes
1 cup cantaloupe, diced
1 cup watermelon, diced
1 cup cucumber, seeded and
  diced
⅓ cup red onion, chopped
1 teaspoon jalapeno, seeded
  and minced
2 tablespoons fresh lime juice

2 tablespoons cilantro, coarsely
  chopped
4 boneless chicken breasts
4 fried tortilla shells (can be
  purchased at specialty
  stores)
1 head crisp lettuce leaves
1 cup commercial
  honey-mustard dressing

In medium glass bowl, mix tomatoes, cantaloupe, watermelon, cucumber, onion, jalapeno, lime juice, and cilantro together. Refrigerate for at least 1 hour. Grill chicken breasts approximately 5 to 7 minutes on each side or until done. Remove from heat and slice. Divide ingredients into 4 equal portions. Arrange a layer of lettuce leaves in bottom of tortilla shell and top with a layer of fruit salsa and chicken slices. Serve with honey-mustard dressing on the side. Serves 4.

The Garden Cafe

250 Madison Avenue
YUMA

$\mathscr{H}$alf the fun of dining at the historic Garden Cafe lies in getting there. A winding brick path leads from a streetside courtyard entrance through wrought-iron gates and past quaint shops, aviaries, and flowering vines. When you finally arrive at the enchanting, open-air restaurant at the end of the walk, you'll feel as if you've discovered a secret garden. Leafy shade trees and a bright tri-colored canopy provide a roof for the three brick dining terraces. The heady fragrance of lemon trees and birds chirping in room-sized cages add an effect bordering on magical in this delightful outdoor environment.

The restaurant and adjoining coffee shop are in the former garage and backyard of the E.F. Sanguinetti residence located next door. The home, which featured one of the areas first swimming pools, is said to date back to the 1870s. It was built by the illustrious Mr. Sanguinetti, a successful Yuma businessman with interests in mining, dairying, ranching, and farming. The original residence was converted into a museum in 1963, but a portion of the grounds and some adjoining buildings are still operated by family members. The outdoor cafe is the most recent family venture and, perhaps, the most charming.

I'm not sure whether it was the flora, fauna, or crisp mid-day air that aroused my appetite. Most likely it was the heavenly aromas drifting over from a nearby table. The tempting sights and smells belonged to the cafe's daily special, Tortilla Soup and Southwestern Quiche. There was no doubt in my mind or on my palate. I had to have it.

Breakfast
9:00 A.M. until 11:00 A.M.
Tuesday through Friday

8:00 A.M. until 11:30 A.M.
Saturday

Sunday Brunch
8:00 A.M. until 2:30 P.M.

Lunch
11:00 A.M. until 2:30 P.M.
Tuesday through Friday

Noon until 2:30 P.M.
Saturday

Closed Monday

For reservations
call (520) 783-1491

When the friendly "garden girl" arrived with my lunch, I knew at once that my choice was the right one. The tomato-based, lightly spiced soup arrived brimming with tortilla strips, avocado, sour cream, and jack cheese. This soup could have been a meal in itself. The tasty quiche was exactly as I had hoped it would be, thick and cheesy with a gentle green-chile kick. Next time I'll order the Pollo Plate, a heavenly chicken salad, that is listed on a menu featuring a variety of sandwiches, soups, salads, and desserts.

There's a story at The Garden Cafe about how the restaurant's patrons demanded that the Chocolate Killer Cake become a regular item on the menu. After hearing the tale, I ordered a piece to find out what all the fuss was about. Let it be said that this wonderful chocolate confection proves, once again, that the customer is always right. In fact, the staff has taken it a step farther and now packages the cake mix for sale. Stop in the cafe's gift shop and pick up the pre-packaged ingredients, or follow the recipe on the following page. Be careful though, or your family and friends may insist that it become a regular in your kitchen.

The Garden Cafe's Tortilla Soup

2 tablespoons butter or butter
  substitute
1 cup onion, chopped
1 clove garlic, finely diced
1/3 cup tomato juice
6 cups chicken broth
1 tablespoon crushed mild
  chilies

3 cups corn tortilla chips
1½ cups Monterey Jack
  cheese, grated
1 cup sour cream
chives
sliced avocado for garnish

Melt butter in soup pot over medium heat. Add onion and garlic and sauté until onions are transparent, about 2 minutes. Add tomato juice, chicken broth, and chilies. Heat over low heat for 30 to 35 minutes. To serve, place ½ cup tortilla chips in each of 6 bowls. Pour soup over chips and sprinkle ¼ cup grated cheese over each serving. Top with dollop of sour cream, pinch of chives, and slice of avocado. Serves 6.

The Garden Cafe's Southwestern Quiche

1 cup flour
¼ teaspoon salt
½ cup shortening
¼ cup water
vegetable-oil spray
2 eggs
½ cup whipping cream
½ cup half-and-half

¼ teaspoon pepper
½ cup diced canned chilies
½ cup sliced black olives
¾ cup Monterey Jack cheese,
  shredded
¾ cup long horn cheese,
  shredded

Combine flour, salt, shortening, and water in bowl. Mix together and form dough into ball. Spray vegetable oil on 9-inch pie pan. Pat dough into pan and form into pie shell. In separate bowl, combine eggs, whipping cream, half-and-half, pepper, chilies, olives, and cheeses. Mix ingredients well and pour into shell. Bake in 350-degree oven for 35 to 40 minutes.

The Garden Cafe's Chocolate Killer Cake

2 cups water
1 cup (2 sticks) butter,
  softened
1½ cups sugar
2 eggs

2 tablespoons vanilla
2 cups flour
2 teaspoons baking powder
2 teaspoons baking soda
⅔ cup cocoa

Heat water and butter together in saucepan or in microwave until butter is melted. Combine remaining ingredients in large bowl. Add water-butter mixture and mix on high speed of electric mixer for approximately 2 minutes until well blended. Pour into 9- by 13-inch prepared pan and bake in 350-degree oven for 35 to 40 minutes. Do not open oven door until done. Allow cake to cool before frosting. Serves 8.

Cream Cheese Frosting

3 ounces cream cheese, softened
¼ cup (½ stick) butter, softened

1 teaspoon vanilla
2½ cups powdered sugar

Combine cream cheese and butter in bowl. Mix at medium speed until well blended, about 1 minute. Add vanilla and powdered sugar, mixing well. Spread onto cool cake.

P. Paris

Li'l Abner's Steakhouse

8500 North Silverbell Road
MARANA

$\mathcal{L}$i'l Abner's Steakhouse is located at a former stop on the Butterfield Express stage line, which rumbled across Arizona in the mid-1800s. If the steakhouse had been in operation at the stage stop during that time, there's no telling how many passengers would have decided to end their journey at the stop and settle nearby. The aroma of mesquite-smoked steaks sizzling over an open fire might have been too tempting to leave behind.

5:00 P.M. until 10:00 P.M.
Sunday through Thursday

5:00 P.M. until 11:00 P.M.
Friday and Saturday

For reservations
call (520) 744-2800

The aged, adobe-brick building that today houses Li'l Abner's Steakhouse reportedly dates back to the early 1900s. The structure served for many years as an eyeglass factory before it was converted into a restaurant and expanded. Supposedly, a restless ghost still wanders through the rooms of the old factory searching for a lost pair of spectacles. Then again, maybe the spirit is reluctant to leave the entertaining setting at this rustic restaurant, which looks much like a scene from an old cowboy movie.

Li'l Abner's was established in 1947 and has been going strong ever since. Located in the desert about fifteen miles north of downtown Tucson, Li'l Abner's is everything an old western steakhouse should be—rowdy, rustic, and relaxed. The best way to find the steakhouse is to let your nose be your guide. When you smell the mesquite burning, you're almost there. No fancy duds are needed here, just a pair of broken-in jeans and a cowboy hat and you'll feel like one of the crowd. Everyone knows that cowboys of the Old West favored steak and beans cooked outdoors over an open fire. Li'l Abner's upholds that tradition for the cowboys of today.

A wooden picnic table on the large outdoor patio is a great spot for dining in the evening under Arizona's clear and starry skies. It's also the best place to watch the chef tossing steaks on the open pit barbecue. If you'd rather dine indoors, step inside the restaurant's smoke-filled interior where you'll find enough graffiti and cowboy paraphernalia on the walls and ceiling to keep you entertained for hours.

On the night I visited Li'l Abner's, the roaring fire in the old stone fireplace took away the chill of the February evening, and the smell of steaks on the grill aroused my appetite. Ordering dinner is a simple affair. There are no written menus, just friendly servers in fringed shirts ready to take your order for a seven-ounce filet mignon, one-pound T-bone, or two-pound porterhouse. And yes, there are also chicken and ribs, which get the same mesquite-grilled treatment as the main draw. A bottle of cold beer washes it all down with ease. Since there's so much to wash down, what with salad and all the pinto beans, garlic bread, and salsa you can handle, you may need a couple of brews to go with your dinner.

Such generous dinner portions usually leave little room for dessert, but if you can't imagine a meal without a sweet ending, there's always ice cream. If you're a country music fan, you'll enjoy the lively background music, but if it's the real thing you want, plan to be here on Friday and Saturday nights when a country-western band really livens things up. Who can blame the old spectacle-searching spirit for refusing to leave this fun-loving atmosphere?

Li'l Abner's Steakhouse's Salsa

1 large can (28 ounces) whole tomatoes, chopped, or 4 fresh tomatoes, chopped
1 small onion, chopped
1 can (4 ounces) green chilies, diced

pepper to taste
1 tablespoon garlic, minced (optional)
2 to 3 tablespoons cilantro, chopped (optional)

If using canned tomatoes, do not drain. Combine all ingredients in medium bowl and stir to blend. Cover and refrigerate. Serve as a dip for tortilla chips, use as a vegetable side dish, or pour over pinto beans before or after cooking. Makes approximately 4 cups.

Li'l Abner's Steakhouse's "Hitching Post Stumbler" Margarita

salt
2 ounces Cuervo Gold Tequila
½ ounce Grand Marnier
5 ounces sweet-and-sour mix

½ ounce fresh lime juice
½ to ¾ cup crushed ice
lime slice for garnish

Dampen rim of an oversized Margarita glass and dip in salt. Set aside. In blender container, combine tequila, Grand Marnier, sweet-and-sour mix, lime juice, and ice. Blend for approximately five seconds at low speed. Then blend at high speed for a few more seconds. Pour into salt-rimmed glass and garnish with lime slice. Makes 1 very generous drink.

Arizona Inn

2200 East Elm Street
TUCSON

When the Arizona Inn opened in 1930, it was heralded as a quiet, isolated desert retreat far away from downtown Tucson. Today, after a sixty-plus-year reign as Tucson's oldest resort and one of the Southwest's most elegant hideaways, this gracious landmark sits right in the middle of a residential neighborhood in the city's midtown area. The fact that the town's sprawl enclosed the Arizona Inn hasn't hampered the luxurious feeling of seclusion that still exists at this cloistered 14-acre retreat. But that, of course, is just the way Isabella Greenway planned it.

Greenway, the dynamo who created the Arizona Inn, was a shrewd businesswoman, an active community leader, and a popular hostess, as well as Arizona's first congresswoman. Her purpose for founding the inn was twofold. She wanted to create a private refuge for her well-heeled friends, many of whom were celebrities (Isabella was one of Eleanor Roosevelt's bridesmaids), and she wanted to establish a customer for her furniture factory that employed World War I veterans recuperating from illness in the desert climate. Many original pieces of handcrafted furniture from the factory are used today at the inn, which is still owned and managed by members of the Greenway family.

The Arizona Inn's handsome, sunken dining room, with beamed ceilings and a rustic beehive fireplace, offers an inviting setting in which to dine, especially during winter evenings when a classical guitarist entertains. But I arrived in the middle of the day, so I chose a seat on the outdoor patio overlooking the resort's impeccably manicured gardens. From my table under a cobalt-blue awning, I could see flower beds blooming in a kaleidoscope of colors, neatly trimmed lawns, and winding garden paths leading to clusters of bright coral-

Breakfast
7:00 A.M. until 10:30 A.M.
Daily

Lunch
11:30 A.M. until 2:00 P.M.
Daily

Dinner
5:00 P.M. until 10:00 P.M.
Daily

Sunday Brunch
11:00 A.M. until 2:00 P.M.

Jackets are suggested for men.

For reservations
(recommended)
call (520) 325-1541

pink stucco cottages. It was the perfect place for enjoying one of the historic inn's meals.

The menu changes with the seasons at this celebrated inn which recently added the "Silver Spoon" award to its impressive list of dining distinctions. The kitchens at the inn have long been recognized for their continental cuisine enhanced by flavors of the Southwest. I was glad the season was right for the savory chilled Gazpacho, the mildly spiced Quesadilla, and the delectable Roasted Poblano Chile stuffed with tender chicken and goat cheese. Feeling like celebrating amidst all the pampering and floral splendor, I raised my glass of Sauvignon Blanc—a product of Southwest Cellars, one in the growing colony of Arizona vineyards—and toasted the imaginative and resourceful Isabella Greenway for creating this splendid inn.

I took the long way out, meandering past nineteenth-century Audubon prints in the airy, dome-ceilinged lounge and past Mrs. Greenway's collection of African safari relics and Spanish-colonial antiques. Given the gorgeous surroundings, it didn't surprise me a bit to learn that the Arizona Inn, which is listed on the National Register of Historic Places, is a favorite setting for local weddings and celebrations. It also didn't surprise me to learn that many of the inn's guests have been spending their winter vacations here for over three generations.

Arizona Inn's Quesadilla

2 flour or corn tortillas
¼ cup melted butter or olive oil
⅓ cup aged cheddar cheese, shredded
⅓ cup Monterey Jack cheese, shredded

1 small tomato, diced
1 small scallion, chopped
4 to 5 sprigs cilantro, chopped

Heat large skillet over medium-high heat. Brush tortilla with butter on one side and place it in pan, buttered side down. Sprinkle shredded cheeses on tortilla. Add remaining ingredients. Butter second tortilla on one side and place on top, butter side up. When bottom tortilla has browned, turn over and brown on other side. May be served topped with salsa, guacamole, and/or sour cream. Serves 1 or 2.

Arizona Inn's Smoked Quail

½ cup balsamic vinegar
¼ cup lime juice
1 teaspoon cracked
  black pepper
kosher salt to taste
4 quails, rinsed and dried
1 cup dry bread crumbs, cubed
1 cup green apples, chopped
¼ cup chicken stock
1 cup pecan halves

¼ cup brown sugar
2 tablespoons red chili powder
¼ cup water
4 cups apple cider
1 cinnamon stick
1 clove
1 clove garlic, minced
1 pint whipping cream
¼ cup apple brandy

Prepare marinade by combining balsamic vinegar, lime juice, black pepper, and salt in large flat-bottomed dish. Add quail and marinate for 2 hours. In bowl, combine bread crumbs, apples, and chicken stock. Place in buttered pan and bake at 350 degrees for a half hour until brown. In separate bowl, mix together pecan halves, brown sugar, red chili powder, and water. In small saucepan, cook pecan mixture over medium heat until all water is gone and sugar has caramelized. Remove from heat and cool. Add pecans to bread stuffing mixture and blend well. Set aside and keep warm. In sauté pan, mix together cider, cinnamon stick, clove, and garlic. Heat and reduce to 1 cup. Strain sauce and add whipping cream. Reduce mixture to original volume of 1 cup. Add brandy and cook over low heat for 10 minutes. Set aside and keep warm.

Soak wood barbecue chips overnight. Preheat half of gas barbecue grill on low and add wood chips. Place quail on cool side of grill and close top. Cook until done, approximately 20 to 30 minutes. Check often. Spread warm stuffing on plate. Place quail on top and cover with apple brandy sauce. Serves 2.

Carlos Murphy's

419 West Congress Street
TUCSON

$\mathcal{A}$s soon as you lay eyes on the massive old train depot that is now the home of Carlos Murphy's, you know that this was no ordinary railroad terminal. Construction on the handsome granite structure began in 1912, when the El Paso and Southwestern Railroad extended its rail lines from El Paso, Texas, to Tucson. When work was completed in 1915, the two-story de-

11:00 A.M. until 10:00 P.M.
Sunday through Thursday

11:00 A.M. until 11:00 P.M.
Friday and Saturday

For reservations
call (520) 628-1956

pot featured a giant rotunda with a stained-glass dome, electric lights, running water, and the city's first toilet facilities located in a commercial structure. A park with shade trees and decorative fountains was added to separate the passenger trains from the freight tracks, making the depot an elegant cut above Arizona's early wooden train stations.

In 1981 the cavernous landmark became Carlos Murphy's, a restaurant specializing in authentic Mexican food and an entertaining atmosphere. The idea here is to have fun along with your meal, and there are plenty of diversions guaranteed to take your mind off more serious subjects. The old brick walls and tiled floor help to keep the old depot's past alive, but the Mexican biplane, the punching bag, and a brightly painted canoe dangling from the lofty ceilings may have you thinking more of a Mexican circus than a historic landmark. However, that is what you can expect at a place where a sign by the front door reads, "Open: When we feel like it. Close: When we have to."

The menu here is as much fun as the surroundings, and it supplies detailed descriptions of many of the restaurant's specialties. My order of Combination Fajitas, a do-it-yourself plateful featuring sizzling marinated strips of beef and chicken with vegetables, warm tortillas, and plenty of Mexican trimmings, looked like it could have fed half the Mexican army. Since Southwesterners and the staff at this restaurant take their Margaritas seriously, I ordered an Acapulco Goldrush from the bar, located in the former garage where trains were parked and serviced at the depot. Let me say that the restaurant's claim is true, the smooth, mellow, tequila-based wonder will win enthusiasm from even the toughest Margarita critic. Other house specialties—prepared in a kitchen occupying an area where trains once ran—include the Grilled Fish Tacos, the "Best of Mexico" Chimichanga, and a variety of Mexican combination plates. I chuckled when I came across the most talked-about item on the menu, the Iwanna Iguana Tacos, available only in iguana season which runs from February 30 to 31.

If there's room left for dessert, a separate menu at your table lists Carlos' Sweet Sensations. However, be forewarned. If all of the selections are as hefty as the Monster Cookie, you may have to call in the Mexican army.

Carlos Murphy's Combination Fajitas

1 pound chicken breast
1 pound sirloin steak
¼ cup lemon juice
¼ cup lime juice
½ cup vegetable oil
½ cup beer
3 cloves garlic, minced
½ teaspoon ground cumin
½ teaspoon ground red chile
1 red bell pepper, seeded and sliced
1 green bell pepper, seeded and sliced
1 medium onion, sliced
1 tomato, seeded and sliced
½ teaspoon salt
½ teaspoon pepper
1 tablespoon fresh cilantro, chopped or 1 teaspoon dried cilantro
4 to 6 large flour tortillas, warm
salsa, grated cheese, and sour cream for garnish

Arrange chicken and steak in shallow rectangular pan. In separate bowl, mix lemon juice, lime juice, ¼ cup oil, beer, garlic, cumin, and red chile. Pour over meat and marinate in refrigerator for 4 to 6 hours. Remove meat from marinade and grill over hot coals 5 to 7 minutes on each side, or until done. Pour remaining ¼ cup oil into large sauté pan or skillet. Add peppers, onion, tomato, salt, pepper, and cilantro. Stir-fry mixture for 2 to 3 minutes until hot and tender but still crisp. Slice meat against grain into narrow strips. To serve, divide beef, chicken, and vegetables into four equal portions and arrange on plate with a warm tortilla. Garnish with salsa, grated cheese, and sour cream. Serves 4 to 6.

Carlos Murphy's Monster Cookie

1 giant (12-inch diameter)
  commercial chocolate chip
  cookie
1 quart vanilla ice cream
1 bottle chocolate fudge sauce
3 cups whipped cream

1 package (3 to 4 ounces)
  sliced almonds
1 bottle chocolate sprinkles
1 maraschino cherry

Place giant cookie on large serving plate. Place 3 large scoops ice cream (about 1 cup each) on cookie, and top with 1 scoop of ice cream to make a pyramid. Pour chocolate fudge sauce over top and let drizzle to bottom of plate. Frost pyramid with whipped cream. Sprinkle with almonds and chocolate sprinkles and top with cherry. Serves 3 to 4.

Carlos Murphy's Acapulco Goldrush Margarita

1½ ounces Cuervo Gold
  Tequila
½ ounce Grand Marnier
1 ounce fresh lime juice

4 to 6 ice cubes
1 slice lime
salt

In shaker container, pour in tequila, Grand Marnier, lime juice, and ice cubes. Shake until well blended. Rub rim of glass with lime rind. Dip glass in salt to coat rim. Pour shaker ingredients into glass and serve. Makes 1 drink.

El Charro Cafe

311 North Court Avenue
TUCSON

*I*ncredible as it may sound, every morning fifty pounds of beef are hoisted in a metal cage onto the roof of the El Charro Cafe to dry in the sun. The process is said to properly prepare the meat for the restaurant's famous Carne Seca. This dedication to authenticity should give you some idea of how this interesting cafe—which claims to be "the oldest Mexican restaurant in continuous opera-

11:00 A.M. until 9:00 P.M.
Sunday through Thursday

11:00 A.M. until 10:00 P.M.
Friday and Saturday

For reservations
(recommended)
call (520) 622-1922

tion by the same family in the United States"—has maintained its popularity for over seventy years.

Now a National Historic Landmark, the building was constructed by Jules Flin as a home for his family. Flin, a French stonemason whose ghost is said to still roam the house, built the structure out of black-lava rock taken from nearby "A" Mountain. In 1922, Flin's oldest daughter, the widowed and penniless Monica, transformed the family home into a restaurant, naming it after the dashing Mexican horsemen, *los charros*. The energetic and resourceful Monica, considered to be Tucson's first businesswoman, continued to run the restaurant well into her eighties. Today, Monica's grandniece, Carlotta, and her family operate the colorful cafe where Monica's original recipes are still carefully followed.

The cafe's location in Tucson's El Presidio Historic District makes this restaurant a favorite luncheon spot for tourists as well as the downtown business crowd. Businesspeople and tourists alike enjoy the cozy, appealing atmosphere at the restaurant. The wooden floors at the El Charro Cafe are well-worn, and the decor borders on the bizarre with its potpourri of family photos, religious holy card images, Latin love scenes, and old calendars. It's almost like visiting Mexico without having to cross the border.

If you ask the cafe's regular customers, they'll probably tell you the best dish in the house is the famous Carne Seca. Once the sun-dried beef descends to the restaurant's kitchen, it is shredded, spiced, marinated, and sautéed. The tasty concoction appears in a variety of dishes on the jam-packed menu. Who is to argue with Tucsonians who claim

162

this item as their own? Certainly not me. Anxious to try this Tucson delicacy, I ordered my Carne Seca straight with a tortilla on the side and, of course, the standard Mexican accompaniments of beans and rice. To go with the chips and spicy salsa that were served before dinner, I ordered a cold bottle of Arizona's own Chile Beer, although the cafe's excellent homemade wine-based Sangria was also tempting.

The chewy, flavorful, and perfectly spiced shredded beef was everything it promised to be. I asked for the recipe, but I doubt if most people would want to hoist meat onto the roof of their homes. Instead, I was mercifully granted the recipe for Machaca, which doesn't involve any rooftop drying but is said to be a suitable at-home substitute for the restaurant's most famous dish.

Since all the recommended dishes so far had been winners, I went along with the suggested dessert. I was rewarded for my compliancy with a tasty dish of Flan, a slippery slice of egg custard swimming in a pool of Kahlúa-laced caramel sauce, yet another house specialty at the El Charro Cafe.

This is one of those places you can't wait to come back to. I plan to return for the chimichangas, said to have originated here, and for the tamales, chili rellenos, enchiladas, and practically everything else on the menu. Or I may just return to enjoy the cozy feeling in this old home and to watch fifty pounds of beef being hoisted onto the roof.

El Charro Cafe's Machaca

1 cup green chilies, chopped
½ teaspoon salt
½ teaspoon pepper
½ white onion, sliced
  into rings
2 tomatoes, chopped
3 quarts water

4 heads garlic
1 cup water
4 pounds beef brisket,
  chuck or eye of round
juice from 2 limes
¹/₃ cup oil

In large stock pot (8 quarts), bring 3 quarts of water to boil. Make garlic purée by separating garlic heads into cloves. Peel garlic and place in blender container. Add 1 cup water and purée. Drain purée. (Leftover purée can be stored in refrigerator in tightly closed glass jar for as long as a week.) When water reaches boiling point in stock pot, add ¼ cup garlic purée and meat. Return to boil. Skim residue, reduce heat, and simmer about 2 hours until meat is tender. Remove meat and set aside. When cool enough to handle, use fingers to shred meat along grain into strips ½-inch wide. Preheat oven to 325 degrees. Spread shredded meat in single layer on large cookie sheet. Mix lime juice with 1 teaspoon garlic purée and sprinkle over meat. Roast meat until brown, about 15 minutes, stirring occasionally. Drain juices and reserve. Heat oil in large skillet. Sauté chilies with salt and pepper. Add onion and tomatoes and sauté briefly. Add garlic purée and meat, stirring over medium heat to brown. If too dry, moisten with reserved meat juices. May be served alone or as a filler for taco, tortillas, etc. Serves 8 to 10 generously.

El Charro Cafe's Flan

¾ cup granulated sugar
6 eggs, lightly beaten
a pinch of salt
1 teaspoon vanilla extract

1 quart milk
1 cup whipping cream
dash Kahlúa liqueur
slivered almonds for garnish

Caramelize ½ cup sugar by heating in skillet over very low heat. Stir constantly until sugar melts and turns brown. Do not burn. Spread caramel in 1½-quart shallow baking dish (can be any shape) and set aside. In bowl combine eggs, remaining sugar, salt, and vanilla extract, beating well with wire whisk. Scald milk and whisk into egg mixture. Strain into baking dish over caramelized sugar. Place baking dish into a roasting pan and place enough hot water in roasting pan to come halfway up sides of baking dish. Bake at 350 degrees for 20 to 30 minutes, or until knife inserted into center comes out clean. Allow to cool on wire rack until lukewarm. Cover and refrigerate until chilled. In mixing bowl, whip cream with dash or two of Kahlúa. When ready to serve, slice flan into squares. Loosen edges of custard with spatula and invert onto serving plate. Caramel will flow over custard. Top each serving with a dollop of whipped cream and sprinkle with slivered almonds. Yields 8 to 12 servings.

Janos

150 North Main Street
TUCSON

*D*iscovering Janos is like uncovering a rare jewel. The building's unassuming facade disguises the fact that behind the thick white walls and closed blue shutters lies one of Tucson's most celebrated restaurants.

Janos is located in a building in the El Presidio District, a historic section of Tucson that dates back to the 1770s when the town was a walled fort. The building is a combination of two former residences. The oldest, built in the mid-1800s, once belonged to a feisty, gun-slinging marshall named Duffield. The other residence, constructed a decade later, was the home of Hiram Stevens, a prominent businessman and politician. After Duffield's death, his house was purchased by Stevens, who combined it with his own home to create a large, elegant residence. The spacious home, which included aviaries, orchards, and stables, served as a social center for nineteenth-century Tucson.

The residence was converted into an exquisite restaurant in 1983, but the gracious hospitality that captivated visitors a century ago still exists at the former Stevens estate. The owners, noted chef Janos (pronounced Yanos) Wilder and his wife Rebecca, have cleverly enhanced the building's historical character by keeping the furnishings and decorating to a minimum. The result is a stunning triumph of elegant simplicity. The thick adobe walls are for the most part unadorned, except when used to display original works by local artists. The old wood-planked floors, cactus-ribbed ceilings, and peach-tinted rooms add a sense of drama to the restaurant and provide a perfect showcase for the highly acclaimed cuisine.

The restaurant's French-inspired southwestern dishes have earned the talented chef a strong local following and numerous regional and national culinary honors, including awards from the prestigious James

Dinner
5:30 P.M. until 9:30 P.M.
Monday through Saturday

Closed Sunday
Closed Monday in summer months

Jackets are suggested
(but not necessary) for men.

For reservations
(recommended)
call (520) 884-9426

Beard Foundation and, for six consecutive years, a Mobil Four-Star Award.

A chef who has received so many accolades is bound to have a repertoire of culinary tricks up his sleeve, and the menu here is testimony to Janos's creative skills. Actually there are two menus. One changes daily and features some of the chef's newest inventions. The other is a seasonal menu with detailed descriptions of some of the restaurant's more familiar dishes. The dishes at Janos have long, intriguing titles like Wild Mushroom and Smoked Poblano Flan, or Grilled Rabbit with Roasted Pepper Purée and Blue Corn Fritters. After looking over the list of selections, I chose the Lobster and Brie-stuffed Chile Relleno as an appetizer, the Opal Basil Vinaigrette for my salad, and Lamb Medallions with Corn Soufflé as my entrée.

As expected, each dish was an outstanding success, perfectly prepared and artistically presented. Attentive servers offer just the right amount of pampering without hovering and provide expert assistance in selecting from the restaurant's impressive wine list. Prepare for a battle with whatever will power you have left when the dessert tray arrives carrying an array of irresistible delights. If you do succumb to the Marquise au Chocolat with Crème Anglaise, don't worry. You can walk off a few calories with a guided tour of this National Historic Landmark—a service the staff provides with pride and with pleasure.

Janos's Smoked Salmon Spirals

4 ounces cream cheese
2 tablespoons fresh dill
juice from one lemon
4 slices smoked salmon

2 tablespoons caviar,
American Golden or
Flying Fish preferred

Combine cream cheese, dill, and lemon juice in blender container or food processor container and purée. Lay each slice of smoked salmon on sheet of plastic wrap. Spread salmon lightly with cream cheese spread. Top with layer of caviar. Roll in a jelly-roll style and secure tightly with plastic wrap. Refrigerate for several hours. Slice into spirals. Makes 12 appetizer servings.

Janos's El Presidio Chicken Croquettes

8 chicken breasts,
  boneless and skinless
3 egg whites
2 Anaheim chilies, roasted,
  peeled, seeded and
  finely diced
1½ cups cheddar cheese, grated
3 tomatoes, peeled, seeded
  and finely diced

6 scallions, finely diced
1½ tablespoons fresh garlic,
  finely chopped
3 tablespoons fresh cilantro,
  roughly chopped
¾ cup heavy cream
salt and pepper to taste

Breading

3 cups flour
1½ cups milk
4 cups coarse dry bread
  crumbs

½ to 1 cup cooking oil
  or shortening

Cut chicken into chunks and put in food processor container. Add egg whites and process quickly until chicken is coarsely chopped. Do not purée, as chicken should be fairly coarse. Pour into bowl and fold in chilies, cheese, tomatoes, scallions, garlic, cilantro, and cream. Season with salt and pepper. Shape mixture into 16 round patties about ½-inch thick. Set out individual containers of flour, milk, and bread crumbs. Dust each croquette with flour. Dip gently in milk, then coat with bread crumbs, handling carefully so croquettes maintain their shape. Preheat oven to 350 degrees. Heat ½-inch oil or shortening in medium or large sauté pan. Add croquettes and fry over medium heat until golden brown, turning once. Add additional oil or shortening if needed. Place on cookie sheet and finish in oven until thoroughly cooked, about 20 minutes. Allow 2 croquettes per serving. Serves 8.

Debbi Hampton

Samaniego Place Grill and Bar

110 South Church Avenue
TUCSON

11:00 A.M. until 11:00 P.M.
Monday through Saturday

For reservations
(recommended for dinner)
call (520) 884-9420

The attractive pink adobe building in downtown Tucson that houses the Samaniego Place Grill and Bar is said to date from the 1860s, the time when Tucson was enjoying its lofty status as capital of the newly formed Arizona Territory. The 1860s were Wild-West years in Tucson, a time when shootouts erupted in dusty streets and gambling halls thrived. But by the time the capital was moved northward to Phoenix a few decades later, the once-rowdy Tucson was well on its way to becoming a refined city.

Located near the heart of the city, the historic town house known today as Samaniego Place Grill and Bar was once the residence of Mariano Samaniego, a wealthy rancher, stage-line owner, and well-known local politician and civic figure. The energetic Samaniego served on numerous boards, was a delegate to the territorial legislature, a regent of the University of Arizona, and a two-term president of the Arizona Pioneers' Historical Society. No doubt, his adobe home was the scene of frequent gatherings for Tucson's elite. The Mexican-born Samaniego also retained a deep respect for his native country's traditions, and his efforts to preserve and promote the cultural identity of the town's Spanish-speaking community made him a popular figure in the "Old Pueblo," the local nickname for Tucson.

After it was used as a home, the structure served a stint as the Old Pueblo Men's Club and then suffered through a twenty-year period of dormancy before it was converted into a restaurant. Today, more than a century later, the old Samaniego residence continues to occupy a prominent spot in Tucson's vibrant downtown area. Located next door to the Tucson Convention Center, a major exhibition-and-entertainment complex, the restaurant is a favorite dining spot for conventioners, concert fans, and patrons of the arts.

The building's rustic charm is evident throughout the restaurant's dining areas in the original rooms of the house. The furnishings are simple and beautifully complement the three-foot-thick adobe walls and rugged cactus-ribbed ceilings. Framed black-and-white photos on the walls provide a glimpse into Arizona's past. A spacious bar-

and-lounge area has been added to the original structure and features large windows overlooking the manicured grounds of the Convention Center. Two inviting, flower-studded patios provide alfresco dining and an opportunity to sharpen your people-watching skills.

Like the restaurant's architecture and decor, the menu is unpretentious and uncomplicated. It lists sandwiches, entrées, pasta, salads, and dessert selections while the daily specials appear on a blackboard near the entrance. The cuisine is familiar and traditional, including a few dishes featuring the chile-spiked flavors of the Southwest. After being informed by both the owner and the chef that the Southwestern-Style Grilled Chicken Breast—appearing on the menu as a sandwich and an entrée—was the current favorite among the diners, I decided to follow the crowd. The plump and juicy grilled chicken breast covered with green chilies and hot pepper cheese had my taste buds dancing. When my dining companion and cousin, Sharon, a Tucsonian who knows a good thing when she tastes it, insisted that I try a sample of her Red Potato Salad, I gladly obliged. Unable to resist the restaurant's old-world charm and the chef's delicious creations, I abandoned all notions of counting calories and ordered dessert—a White Parisian Truffle with Lemon Sauce. My reward for cleaning the plates set before me was the chef's recipes.

Samaniego Place Grill and Bar's Southwestern-Style Grilled Chicken Sandwich

1 chicken breast, boneless and skinless
2 slices sourdough bread
2 teaspoons mayonnaise
1 can (4 ounces) green chilies, drained
1 thick slice hot pepper cheese
¼ cup quality commercial salsa

Grill chicken breast for approximately 5 minutes on each side until done. While chicken is cooking, toast bread and spread each slice with 1 teaspoon mayonnaise. Add warm, cooked chicken breast. Top with drained chilies and pepper cheese. Heat in microwave for approximately 20 seconds or until cheese begins to melt. Serve with salsa. Makes 1 sandwich.

Samaniego Place Grill and Bar's Red Potato Salad

4 pounds red potatoes, cooked
²/₃ cup mayonnaise
¹/₃ cup Dijon mustard
¹/₂ cup celery, diced
¹/₂ cup onion, diced
¹/₂ cup cucumber, peeled,
   seeded, and diced

3 eggs, hard boiled and
   chopped
¹/₂ teaspoon salt
¹/₂ teaspoon pepper
¹/₄ teaspoon garlic powder

Leave skins on potatoes and dice into ¼-inch pieces. In small bowl, combine mayonnaise and mustard and blend well. In large bowl, mix potatoes, celery, onions, cucumbers, and eggs. Add mayonnaise-mustard mixture and salt, pepper, and garlic powder. Gently toss until potatoes are evenly coated. Serves 4.

Samaniego Place Grill and Bar's
Chicken Breast with Lemon-Butter Sauce

4 chicken breasts, boneless
   and skinless
1 large lemon, peeled
½ small onion, chopped
2 cups white wine

2 cups whipping cream
1 cup (2 sticks) butter
½ teaspoon salt
¼ teaspoon black pepper
¼ teaspoon garlic powder

Grill chicken breasts over high heat until done, approximately 5 minutes on each side. Set aside and keep warm. Cut peeled lemon into quarters and remove seeds. In blender container, combine lemon and onion and blend at high speed for about one minute until smooth. In large saucepan, combine white wine, whipping cream, lemon-onion mixture, butter, salt, pepper, and garlic powder. Mix well and cook over low heat, allowing mixture to reduce by ¼. Arrange ½ cup of sauce on bottom of serving plate and place chicken breast on top. Serves 4.

The Tack Room

2800 North Sabino Canyon Road
TUCSON

*J*f The Tack Room's name evokes images of a rough cowboy steakhouse, you couldn't be farther from the truth. Rather, the white adobe hacienda crowning a secluded hilltop amid a forest of paloverde and mesquite trees is the epitome of southwestern elegance.

Dinner
6:00 P.M. until 9:30 P.M.
Daily

Closed Monday
during the summer

For reservations
(recommended)
call (520) 722-2800

The sprawling, flat-roofed structure was built in 1938 for horse-racing enthusiast Robinson Locke, who wanted a party home overlooking his quarterhorse and sulky racing track. The racing festivities ended a few years later when the property was sold to a family named Grant. The Grants converted the racetrack into a cotton farm and enlarged the house to accommodate their family. Another transformation occurred in the mid-1940s, when the property was sold to a group of investors and developed into a rustic, refined guest ranch. The Rancho Del Rio offered lodging, various activities, and three hot meals a day. Fan and Marvin Kane eventually bought out the Rancho Del Rio's other investors and, in 1952, turned the management of the facility over to their son, Jud. The twenty-two-year-old Jud called upon his favorite cook, his sister Alma Vactor, and the stage was set for a family venture that would last more than forty years and involve three generations.

The restaurant's reputation for fine dining was established during its years as a gourmet dining room reserved for ranch guests. In 1965, the Tack Room, specializing in haute cuisine and superb service, opened to the public. Eight years later, it was the first Arizona restaurant to win the prestigious Mobil Four-Star Award. Since then, the Tack Room has received enough local and national awards to fill a book, placing the restaurant in a class by itself. It currently ranks as the only restaurant in the West to achieve the coveted Mobil Five-Star Award and the American Automobile Association's Five-Diamond Award.

The entrance is located at the back of the restaurant, providing an excellent opportunity to enjoy the exquisitely manicured grounds and gardens. The building's former breezeway, now a spacious entrance lounge with large fireplaces, sets the tone for the understated elegance throughout the restaurant. Three dining rooms are located to the right of the lounge, each beautifully appointed with candlelit tables, attractive wrought-iron chandeliers, and views of the grounds and the nearby Rincon Mountains.

The cuisine is an impressive blend of American, continental, and southwestern. Dinner was announced with the arrival of chilled vegetable appetizers, delicious warm dill rolls, and a cup of savory Chilled Gazpacho Soup. My dining companions, co-owners Alma Vactor and her son Drew, informed me that the menu changes regularly, so I considered myself fortunate to have arrived on an evening when the Open-Faced Ravioli of Roasted Duckling with Cinnamon-Orange Sauce was available. Other exciting entrées available that evening included Rack of Lamb with Mesquite Honey and Lime, Pork Tenderloin Marinated in Mustard and Sour Mash Bourbon, and Sea Scallops in Saffron Broth. After a fruity, palate-cleansing sorbet, which precedes the main course, my companions and I sampled, shared, and saluted the chef's culinary talents, which were equally matched by his artistic presentation. The service by tuxedoed waiters was impeccable. The drama continued all the way through the evening's romantic finale, Chocolate Truffles and long-stemmed roses for the ladies.

The Tack Room's Chilled Gazpacho Soup

1¾ pounds tomatoes, chopped, or 2 cans (14.5 ounces) sliced baby tomatoes
1 can pitted black olives
¾ cup celery, chopped
¾ cup green onions, chopped
¾ cup cucumbers, chopped
2 cloves fresh garlic, minced
3 tablespoons red wine vinegar
1 teaspoon Worcestershire sauce

1½ tablespoons Maggi seasoning
1½ cups beef stock, or 1 can (10½ ounces) beef broth
¾ cup Chablis wine
Tabasco to taste
croutons
chopped chives

Chop tomatoes into small pieces and set aside. Slice olives into thirds. Combine all ingredients except croutons and chives. Chill

175

well for 24 hours. Divide into portions. Serve chilled and garnish with croutons and chopped chives. Serves 4 to 6.

The Tack Room's Steak Tartare

4 anchovy fillets
⅛ tablespoon dry mustard
¼ tablespoon red wine vinegar
1 tablespoon garlic oil
2 dashes Tabasco
2 dashes Worcestershire sauce
1 raw egg yolk
6 ounces raw sirloin or
   tenderloin (no fat),
   finely chopped
2 tablespoons onion, minced

1 tablespoon fresh parsley,
   chopped
1 hard-boiled egg, grated
a dash of cognac or brandy
   (optional)
salt and freshly ground
   pepper to taste
2 tablespoons capers
romaine lettuce leaves
sliced tomatoes
1 to 2 slices rye toast

Reduce anchovy fillets to paste by mashing with 2 forks. In large bowl, add dry mustard, vinegar, garlic oil, Tabasco, and Worcestershire sauce to anchovy paste and blend thoroughly. Add egg yolk and mix. Add chopped meat and blend into mixture. Add minced onion, chopped parsley, grated egg, cognac, salt, and pepper and mix well. Add capers, mixing lightly to avoid crushing. Serve on bed of romaine lettuce and garnish with sliced tomatoes and rye toast. Serves 1.

Tanque Verde Ranch

14301 East Speedway Boulevard
TUCSON

There's nothing like an authentic dude ranch for living out your cowboy and cowgirl fantasies. The Tanque Verde Ranch, a 640-acre spread of desert and foothills at the base of the Rincon Mountains, provides the ideal setting for making those fantasies come true. By the time you complete the winding drive past mesquite trees and cacti to the old ranch house, you'll feel as if you've traveled back to the Old West.

The story of the Tanque Verde Ranch begins in the 1860s, when a rancher from Sonora, Mexico, purchased the property and began construction of a cattle ranch. By the 1930s, cattle ranching began to give way to dude ranching. The Tanque Verde Ranch was among the many ranches that made the change, and it soon began to attract guests looking for western-style vacations from all over the world. Since 1957, the ranch has been owned and operated by the Cote family. They have fashioned the Tanque Verde Ranch into Tucson's most luxurious guest ranch, with a world-wide reputation for gracious western hospitality and gourmet dining.

In the beginning, the excellent gourmet dishes prepared by master chefs were only available to lodgers at the ranch and their guests. However, the food was so good that many a Tucsonian was known to have finagled an invitation to dinner from their snowbirding friends. Eventually, local pressure prevailed, and the dining room was opened to the public.

Some of the ranch's original adobe buildings are still standing. The restaurant is located at the back of the oldest, a territorial-style, tin-roofed building with a wide front porch dating back to 1868. A walk through the century-old ranch house, with its original saguaro-ribbed ceilings, cement floors, and large stone fireplace, leads to the dining rooms which are attached at the rear of the building. Meals are served on the former screened porch, now enclosed, and in the spacious

Breakfast
8:00 A.M. until 9:00 A.M.
Daily

Lunch
Noon until 1:30 P.M.
Daily

Dinner
6:00 P.M. until 8:00 P.M.

For reservations
(preferred)
call (520) 296-6275

main dining room, a recent addition to the building. Wall-to-wall windows in the Sonoran-style main dining room provide a sweeping view of the mountains, the desert, and the swimming pool area complete with a waterfall.

Boots and jeans are proper attire anytime at the ranch, even at meals. It might be wise to loosen the belt a notch, because meals here fall into the "feast" category. Buffet lunches feature a copious selection of everything from soup to nut-filled desserts. With such a glorious bounty spread out before you, it's impossible not to go overboard. Dinner is another gourmet affair. The mesquite grill is lit and the celebrated chef rustles up some glorious grub—including specially-aged steaks, Young Ducklings Glazed with Prickly Pear Syrup, and Barbecued Pork Loin Ribs with Poblano Chili Hush Puppies. Desserts, made on the premises, will dissolve any thoughts of counting either calories or fat grams. Besides, you can work off the excess at the old-fashioned square dance that sometimes follows dinner at the ranch.

Tanque Verde Ranch's Stuffed French Toast

6 slices French bread,
  cut in 1-inch slices
1 package (8 ounces)
  cream cheese
1 tablespoon orange juice
1 teaspoon grated orange rind,
  sour orange preferred
a pinch of sugar
6 eggs, slightly beaten
2 tablespoons cream or milk

a dash of salt
a dash of nutmeg
¼ teaspoon vanilla
2 tablespoons sugar
3 to 4 tablespoons butter
1 jar (8 ounces) commercial
  prickly pear cactus jelly
  or currant jelly
4 tablespoons water
2 teaspoons lemon juice

With small paring knife, cut pocket in middle of each slice of bread, width-wise. In small bowl, combine cream cheese, orange juice, orange rind, and pinch of sugar. Blend well. Fill each bread pocket with generous amount of cheese-orange mixture. Prepare dipping batter by combining eggs, cream, salt, nutmeg, vanilla, and sugar. Blend until sugar is dissolved. Dip stuffed bread slices into batter one at a time, allowing bread to drip for a minute. Melt butter in skillet and fry bread slices in butter over medium heat until golden brown on both sides. Heat jelly in small saucepan. Add 4 tablespoons water and heat until the consistency of syrup. Add 2 teaspoons of lemon juice and stir. Serve jelly mixture with French toast. Serves 6.

Tanque Verde Ranch's Broiled Fillet of Sea Bass Mexicana

3 to 4 pounds of sea bass or
  Mexican cabrilla fillets,
  boneless and skinless
  (Greenland turbot or
  red snapper also work well)
¼ cup butter or margarine
¼ cup olive oil

3 cloves garlic, finely minced
3 tablespoons parsley, minced
2 tablespoons lime juice
salt, white pepper, and
  paprika to taste
avocado sauce (see recipe
  below)

Rinse fillets, pat dry, and place on broiler pan or cookie sheet. Melt butter or margarine in small saucepan. Add olive oil, garlic, minced parsley, and lime juice to butter. Heat until bubbling and remove from heat. Brush fillets generously with butter mixture. Season with salt and white pepper. Sprinkle tops lightly with paprika. Place under broiler or in a 375-degree oven until white and flaky, approximately 20 to 25 minutes depending on thickness of fish. Baste once or twice with butter mixture while cooking. Place fish on serving platter or plate. Put spoon of avocado sauce over top of each fillet. Serves 8.

Avocado Sauce

4 large ripe avocados
4 to 6 tablespoons lime juice
4 tablespoons red onion, minced
2 cloves garlic, minced
2 large tomatoes, peeled,
  seeded, and chopped

1 teaspoon ground coriander
  or 1 tablespoon fresh
  cilantro, chopped
3 drops Tabasco sauce
salt to taste

Peel avocados. Cut in half and remove pits. Place in bowl and mash coarsely with fork, blending in lime juice at the same time. Add onion, garlic, tomatoes, coriander or cilantro, Tabasco, and salt to taste. Mix well. Serve with baked or broiled fish.

Historic Saxon House

308 South Haskell Avenue
WILLCOX

The Willcox area is rich with tales of the Chiricahua Apache and their warrior chiefs Cochise and Geronimo who once claimed the territory as their homeland. For over a quarter of a century, battles raged between the Indians and the incoming settlers, before finally coming to an end in the late 1800s. By then, the former battleground was taking on a new look—one dominated by cattle ranches and cowboys. Today, the old "cow town" of Willcox serves as one of the country's principal cattle-shipping centers.

Life on the ranch gets lonesome at times, and this may be the reason prominent Willcox rancher and politician, Harry Saxon, built a town house in Willcox. Saxon built the pioneer-style adobe residence on Haskell Avenue in 1916. The illustrious Mr. Saxon, whose name appears in the Cowboy Hall of Fame, no longer resides at the broad white structure, now listed on the National Register of Historic Places, but it still bears his name. One of only a few authentic "pioneer homes" still standing in Arizona, the building currently houses the Historic Saxon House restaurant.

The current owners, Bob and Marya Murray, literally blew into town one day in 1981 seeking shelter from a windstorm and recognized the Saxon House's potential as a restaurant. After several years of extensive refurbishing following the guidelines of the period, the enterprising couple finally opened to the grateful public.

One of the first things the Murrays did was fasten a wooden plaque above the entrance inscribed with Gaelic words meaning "A Hundred Thousand Welcomes," and the restaurant's three dining rooms and enclosed front porch are a welcoming sight indeed. Each room glows with individual character and reflects the Murrays' heritage as drivers and breeders of trotting horses in New York. In the Tap Room,

Lunch
11:00 A.M. until 2:00 P.M.
Wednesday through Saturday

Dinner
5:00 P.M. until 9:00 P.M.
Wednesday through Friday

5:00 P.M. until 9:00 P.M.
Saturday

Noon until 8:00 P.M.
Sunday

For reservations
(recommended)
call (520) 384-4478

where a century-old bar transported from New York shares the limelight with the building's original wood floors and fireplace, the mood is casual. The feeling is a bit more formal in the Red Room, named for the shade of scarlet that dominates the room, appearing on the walls, curtains, and carpet. I sat at a table in the paneled, cozy Stable Room, created from an old stable that once accommodated the Murrays' trotting horses.

The restaurant's excellent dishes deserve as much attention as the interesting decor. Marya presides over the kitchen, and her expertise with fresh-from-the-garden herbs and vegetables can transform an ordinary meal into a masterpiece. Luckily for me, I arrived in spring, the season for her Cream of Asparagus Soup. The delicious soup seemed to disappear in a heartbeat. Unfortunately, it was not the season for Marya's acclaimed Pyracantha Chicken, so I had to console myself with the recipe.

The favorite entrée at this restaurant is no surprise. In the heart of cowboy and cattle country, it couldn't be anything other than generous cuts of tender, juicy beef served with creamy horseradish. However, rumor has it that even cowboys occasionally break from tradition at this fine historic restaurant. They seem unable to resist some of Marya's special dishes, like the Red Chili Noodles in Creamy Alfredo Sauce, or the savory chicken dishes prepared with fresh rosemary or apples and raisins.

Historic Saxon House's Pyracantha Chicken

6 chicken breasts, boneless
   and skinless
3 egg whites or 2 eggs
¾ cup seasoned bread crumbs
3 tablespoons oil
½ cup cranberry juice
½ cup water

1 cup pyrancantha jelly
   (recipe follows)
2 teaspoons Worcestershire
   sauce
1 tablespoon lemon zest
1 tablespoon Dijon mustard
2 to 3 cloves garlic, minced

Lightly pound chicken to retard shrinkage. In bowl, beat egg whites or eggs and set aside. Pour bread crumbs into separate bowl and set aside. Dip chicken breasts in egg, then in bread crumbs, coating well. Heat oil in large sauté pan or skillet over medium heat. Add chicken pieces and sauté until golden brown on both sides. In a separate large skillet or sauté pan, combine cranberry juice, water, jelly, Worcestershire sauce, lemon zest, mustard, and garlic. Blend well with whisk. Cook over medium heat for 2 to 3 minutes until smooth. Reduce heat to simmer and add chicken. Cook and baste occasionally, for approximately 10 minutes. Serves 6.

Historic Saxon House's Pyracantha Jelly

3 cups pyrancantha berries
4 cups water
1 cup cranberry juice
juice of 1 lemon

juice of 1 medium grapefruit
1 package (2 ounces)
   powdered pectin
4½ cups sugar

Wash berries and remove stems. In large saucepan, bring water and cranberry juice to boil. Add berries and reduce heat to low. Simmer for 30 minutes. Stir in lemon and grapefruit juices and remove from heat. Strain mixture into separate container and discard berries. Measure liquid and, if necessary, add water to equal 4 cups. Return liquid to pan, add powdered pectin, and stir well. Bring mixture to boil. Stir in sugar and continue to boil for 2 minutes. Remove from heat. Skim foam from top, pour into sterilized jars, and seal. Makes about 5½ cups.

Historic Saxon House's Chocolate Amaretto Mousse

2 tablespoons water
½ ounce (½ square)
   unsweetened chocolate
6 ounces semi-sweet
   chocolate morsels

½ cup butter
4 eggs, separated
1 cup heavy cream
½ cup sugar
1 tablespoon amaretto liqueur

Heat water in saucepan and add chocolate. Stir and cook chocolate until blended. Add butter, cook, and stir until blended. Remove from heat but keep warm. In separate bowl, beat egg yolks and gradually add to hot mixture. Allow to cool. Whip heavy cream and add sugar. In separate bowl, beat egg whites until stiff but not dry. Fold cream, egg whites, and amaretto liqueur into chocolate mixture. Divide mousse into 4 dessert dishes and serve. Serves 4.

Bella Union

401 East Fremont Street
TOMBSTONE

6:00 A.M. until 9:30 P.M.
Daily

For reservations
call (520) 457-3656

*I*n Tombstone, the country's best-known "Old West" town, the legends and real history are so intertwined that it is often difficult to separate fact from fiction. The story of the Bella Union includes both.

The Bella Union is a combination saloon, restaurant, and opera house located at the corner of Fremont and Fourth Streets in a sprawling adobe structure that reportedly dates back to 1881. The building originally housed Tombstone's first post office, along with an assortment of the town's pioneer businesses. At the turn of the century, the people of Tombstone, including the miners, gunslingers, and gamblers, came to this site to collect their mail and conduct other daily business.

According to local legend, a candy store operated by an opium-smoking Chinese merchant named Fu Kee was located next to the post office. In 1907, the luckless shopkeeper was accidently slain in his store by his best friend. The story goes that ever since the event, Fu Kee's ghost wanders about the site. Some say the restless spirit is still looking for his cache of opium pipes, which was discovered buried beneath the old candy store during the building's renovation in the 1940s. These days, the wandering ghost must do his searching in the Bella Union's Victorian dining room, now occupying the site of the candy store.

The bright coral-pink stucco building is named after San Francisco's Bella Union, a palace of pleasure best remembered for its introduction of the naughty, heel-kicking "cancan" to the American West. Destroyed in San Francisco's earthquake of 1906 and reborn in Tombstone in the 1990s, the Bella Union revives the Victorian splendor of the West at the turn of the twentieth century.

The main entrance to the restaurant opens into the saloon area — the former site of the post office. However, "enticing elixirs" are now distributed in the building instead of letters. The dining rooms at Bella Union, each with a distinctive personality, reflect different moods of the Old West. The most formal room is a study in Victorian elegance, featuring velvet drapes, lace curtains, and a stamped-copper ceiling. In the adjoining room, fireplaces and wood-paneled walls, concealing the building's original adobe ones, create a more casual feeling. On the patio, open-air dining under the western sky and steaks sizzling on the open, mesquite pit barbecue create a relaxed mood.

The restaurant's tabloid-style menu entertains and educates with an assortment of old advertisements and news items, the restaurant's bill of fare, and a detailed account of the gunfight at the OK Corral. The account is appropriate since this famous shootout is reenacted regularly at the original site, located a few blocks away.

The Bella Union's cuisine is American, and many old familiar dishes appear on the menu. One of my longstanding favorites is shrimp cocktail. As soon as I felt the tasty tingle of horseradish sauce, I knew I had made the right appetizer choice. It wasn't as easy to select an entrée, so I asked for the chef's recommendation. He suggested the house specialty, the sweet and tangy Chicken Morengo. The dish made such a delicious impression, I begged for the recipe.

Since the chef scored so well in the entrée department, I also left my dessert choice up to him. Not surprisingly, he came through again. The scrumptious, old-fashioned Apple Betty, flavored with cinnamon and topped with vanilla ice cream, was the perfect finale for my meal. The old-time Opera House next door is the place for some entertainment after your meal. Billed as an authentic variety theater of the period, the interior features French crystal chandeliers, an antique bar, and the area's largest hardwood dance floor, perfect for a rollicking rendition of the "cancan."

Bella Union's Chicken Morengo

1 tablespoon butter
6 ounces chicken breast
   tenders, diced
¼ cup red peppers, sliced
¼ cup yellow peppers, sliced
¼ cup green peppers, sliced
¼ cup onions, sliced lengthwise
¼ cup fresh mushrooms, sliced

1 ounce brandy
1 ounce dry white wine
¼ cup brown gravy,
   commercial or homemade
2 tablespoon tomato sauce
2 jumbo tiger shrimp,
   steamed, peeled,
   and deveined

Heat butter in sauté pan over medium-high flame. Add diced chicken and sauté for approximately 3 to 4 minutes. Add peppers, onions, and mushrooms to pan and cook an additional two minutes until vegetables are tender. Add brandy, ignite, and stir ingredients until flame is extinguished. Stir in white wine to deglaze pan. Remove from heat and add brown gravy and tomato sauce. Stir well and place on low flame for about 3 to 4 minutes, or until mixture thickens. Serve mixture in rarebit bowl and top with jumbo shrimp. Serves 1 generously.

Bella Union's Apple Brown Betty

1 cup water
1½ pounds fresh apples,
   peeled, cored, and sliced
1 cup sugar
¾ cup butter
1 tablespoon cinnamon
½ teaspoon nutmeg

¼ cup cornstarch
½ cup cold water
1 cup flour
1 cup rolled oats
1 cup brown sugar
1 quart vanilla ice cream

Place 1 cup water in large saucepan. Add apples and cook over medium heat for approximate 8 to 10 minutes. Do not allow apples to scorch or burn. Add sugar, ¼ cup butter, cinnamon, and nutmeg to apples. Blend cornstarch into cold water and add to apple mixture. Mix all ingredients well and remove from heat. Lightly butter a flat baking dish and place apple mixture in pan. In separate bowl, mix flour, oats, brown sugar, and ½ cup butter together until ingredients are thoroughly moistened. Spread topping over apples and bake in 375-degree oven for 15 to 20 minutes, until topping is browned and apple mixture is thick and bubbling. Cut into serving pieces and top with mound of vanilla ice cream. Serves 8 to 10.

The Nellie Cashman Restaurant

Corner of Fifth Street and Toughnut Street
TOMBSTONE

7:00 A.M. until 9:00 P.M.
Daily

For reservations
call (520) 457-2212

*I*f any Arizona town symbolizes the Old West at its wildest, it's Tombstone. Countless novels and movies have portrayed the town as a rowdy, quarrelsome place where frequent barroom brawls erupted into bloody gunfights in the street. The city was home to perhaps the most famous gunfight of all when Wyatt Earp, Doc Holliday, and the Clanton boys shot it out at the OK Corral in 1881. The legacy of the Old West has been preserved and promoted in Tombstone. Today the city resembles a Western movie set, and visitors love it.

Tombstone is known as "The town too tough to die." Judging from the many ghost towns in the surrounding area, it earned its motto for good reason. Times were tough for the town's early citizens, who managed to survive flooding mines and fires that threatened to destroy the city. Perhaps it was that same brand of grit and determination that enabled an Irish lass named Nellie Cashman to open a hotel and restaurant in Tombstone in 1882.

Lured to Tombstone by stories of the boomtown opportunities made possible by the area's silver mines, the petite and spirited Nellie Cashman worked hard and invested wisely. She endeared herself to the local citizens through her legendary culinary skills and humanitarian efforts. This remarkable woman was a major force behind the founding of the first school, Catholic church, and non-military hospital in Tombstone. A full account of this human dynamo's adventures and accomplishments are listed on the back of the restaurant's menu.

Today, the Nellie Cashman Restaurant is the oldest eating establishment in town. The restaurant is located in the original stucco structure and run by Luxembourg native Anita Skinner and her daughter, Sherry. The Skinners have done their best to preserve the building's original appearance. The open, high-ceilinged dining room with its aged wooden ceiling and stone fireplace, looks much as it did when Nellie was in charge. Mismatched antique furnishings and framed old photos and newspaper clippings create a homey feeling in the room. However, linen-dressed tables, fresh carnations, and classical music remind the diner that this is a civilized place, even though staged shootouts occur regularly around the corner at the OK Corral.

The wonderful aromas drifting in from the restaurant's kitchen immediately ignite the appetite and prompt a survey of the restaurant's fare. Lunchtime offers a perfect opportunity to try one of the popular half-pound burgers, like the Tombstone Burger, which comes topped with green chilies, bacon, and cheese and surrounded by a mountain of fries. If you arrive in time for dinner, perhaps Anita will be serving her celebrated Pork Roast with Brandy Sauce and the sweet and tangy Rhubarb Pie for dessert.

If the weather is right on my next visit, I'll ask for a seat on the side patio beside the old stone fountain, and read again the story of the indomitable Nellie Cashman, whose name, like Tombstone, is too tough to die.

The Nellie Cashman Restaurant's Pork Roast with Brandy Sauce

1 boneless pork loin
  (4 to 6 pounds)
1 cup water
1 cup soy sauce
1 teaspoon fresh garlic, minced
1 teaspoon dried oregano
1 teaspoon dried sweet basil

1 teaspoon dried parsley
3 tablespoons cornstarch
½ cup cold water
1 cup brandy
1 can (12 ounces) whole
  straw mushrooms

Place pork, fat side up, in roasting pan with 2-inch sides. In bowl, combine 1 cup water and soy sauce and pour over meat. Add garlic to fluids in pan. Sprinkle dried herbs over top of meat. Cover pan tightly with foil. Bake in oven at 400 degrees for about 1 to 1½ hours. Remove foil and bake for additional 30 minutes, until clear juice comes out of meat when pierced with fork. Remove from oven. Place meat on cutting board. Put roasting pan with drippings on top of stove and bring to boil over low to medium heat. Mix cornstarch into ½ cup cold water. Add and blend into drippings with wire whisk. When mixture returns to a boil, add brandy and drained mushrooms. Stir mixture and keep warm. Slice meat into ½-inch thick slices and serve with brandy sauce. Makes 10 to 12 generous servings.

The Nellie Cashman Restaurant's Rhubarb Pie

5 cups rhubarb, chopped
1½ cups sugar
½ cup cornstarch
⅓ cup shortening
1½ cups all-purpose flour

3 to 4 tablespoons ice cold
    water
1 tablespoon butter
milk

In medium to large saucepan, add rhubarb and enough water to cover rhubarb. Heat to boiling and cook until rhubarb is tender. Drain rhubarb. Add sugar and cornstarch to rhubarb, mixing until blended. Set aside. In a separate bowl, cut shortening into flour in ¼-inch chunks. Dribble ice water, a tablespoon at a time, over flour mixture and mix with fork until mixture holds together. Divide dough in half. On floured surface, roll half of dough out with rolling pin until it is 2 inches larger than pie pan. Place in greased pie pan and form to edges. Cut off excess dough, leaving about a ½-inch overlap. Fill pie shell with rhubarb mixture. Cut butter into pieces and add to top of rhubarb mixture. Roll out remaining dough into a circle approximately 1 inch larger than pie. Lay over top of pie, fold edges of top crust under bottom crust, and pinch shut. Brush top with milk and cut four 1-inch slits in top. Bake in 400-degree oven for one hour, or until crust is golden brown. Makes one 9-inch or 10-inch pie.

Copper Queen Hotel Dining Room

11 Howell Avenue
BISBEE

When the famous Copper Queen Hotel was built at the turn of the twentieth century, the town of Bisbee was in its heyday. At that time, the picturesque town nestled in the Mule Mountains was the world's largest mining city and claimed a population of over twenty thousand. Stately Victorian buildings lined the streets of the bustling downtown, and around the bend at Brewery Gulch, fifty saloons with an assortment of "shady ladies" provided plenty of entertainment for the miners.

Unlike the flimsy structures found in other boom towns of the Old West, buildings in copper-rich Bisbee were often constructed of brick and built to last. One of the town's finest architectural examples of the boom period is the Copper Queen Hotel, a towering brick structure built in 1902 by the Copper Queen Mining Company. Dominating the center of town, which is located at the bottom of a gulch, the majestic hotel was a center of activity and a favorite stopover for mining officials, politicians, and other traveling celebrities. Teddy Roosevelt, General John "Blackjack" Pershing, and John Wayne are a few of the famous who stayed at the "Queen."

Eventually, large-scale mining operations came to a halt in Bisbee, and by 1970, the town had fallen into a state of disrepair. However, restoration of the old part of town started a few years later. The result of this restoration effort is an area known as "Old Bisbee," which looks much as the town did a century ago. The town's romantic mountainside setting reminds some of a landlocked San Francisco and has become a favorite with filmmakers and sightseers. Many of

Breakfast
7:00 A.M. until 11:00 A.M.
Monday through Friday

Lunch
11:00 A.M. until 2:30 P.M.
Saturday

11:00 A.M. until 4:30 P.M.
Sunday

Dinner
5:30 P.M. until 9:00 P.M.
Monday through Friday

4:30 P.M. until 10:00 P.M.
Saturday

4:30 P.M. until 9:00 P.M.
Sunday

For reservations
(recommended)
call (520) 432-2216

these visitors flock to the recently renovated Copper Queen Hotel for a nostalgic trip back to Bisbee in its prime.

Swinging doors lead from the lobby into the Copper Queen Hotel's spacious dining room where the decor is Victorian and the mood is casual and friendly. Interesting antique furnishings are scattered around the dining area, including a handsome stained-glass partition that once occupied a prominent place in the lobby before it was replaced by a more modern contraption, an elevator.

My meal at the Copper Queen began with a cup of Black Bean Soup, a thick, tasty brew that was spicy enough to draw a tear. My dining companions and I selected different entrées so we could indulge in a bit of sampling. My entrée, Penne Pasta with Feta Cheese, Artichoke Hearts, and Homemade Italian Sausage was served in a light cream sauce laced with fresh oregano. It earned everyone's approval, particularly mine. I enjoyed tasting my companions' Blackened Pork Loin with Tomatillo Salsa Verde and Broiled Shrimp Glazed with a Prickly Pear Barbecue Sauce. The chef's special sauces, which often feature flavors native to the Southwest, can turn an ordinary meal into a masterpiece. Each of us maintained that our particular choice was best, but an undisputed winner is the front terrace. When the weather is nice it offers a chance to enjoy alfresco dining with a view of this historic and charming city.

Copper Queen Hotel Dining Room's Southwestern French Onion Soup

4 tablespoons butter
1½ pounds onions, sliced
1 tablespoon fresh thyme, chopped
1 teaspoon black pepper
⅓ cup cream sherry

4 cups beef bouillon
8 ounces Swiss or Gruyére cheese, shredded
2 cups croutons
2 mild green chilies, julienned
1 teaspoon chili powder

Melt butter in large saucepan. Add onions, thyme, and pepper and sauté until onions are golden brown and tender. Add sherry and beef bouillon, stirring well. Cook over medium heat until hot, about 10 minutes. Pour into individual serving bowls. Divide shredded cheese, croutons, chilies, and chili powder and sprinkle over each serving. Brown under broiler until cheese is melted and brown. Serves 4.

Copper Queen Hotel Dining Room's Tomatillo Salsa Verde

1 large lime
¾ pound tomatillos

2 fresh jalapenos, diced
3 cloves fresh garlic

Peel and section lime and combine with remaining ingredients in food processor container or blender. Process for 1 to 2 minutes until blended. Serve with broiled or grilled chicken or pork. Makes ½ cup.

Copper Queen Hotel Dining Room's Pasta Primavera

1½ tablespoons olive oil
2 cups fresh vegetables, chopped
1 teaspoon fresh garlic, chopped
1 teaspoon shallots, chopped
1 teaspoon basil

1 teaspoon oregano
1 teaspoon thyme
1¹/₂ cups heavy cream
¹/₃ cup Parmesan cheese, grated
salt and white pepper to taste
1 pound pasta, cooked al dente

Heat olive oil in large saucepan over medium heat. Add vegetables, garlic, shallots, basil, oregano, and thyme. Sauté for 1 to 2 minutes. Add cream and cook over low heat until vegetables are al dente and sauce has thickened, about 3 to 5 minutes. Add Parmesan cheese. Season with salt and white pepper. Add cooked pasta and toss until well mixed. Makes 2 large or 4 small servings.

Gadsden Hotel Dining Room

1046 G Avenue
DOUGLAS

$\mathcal{B}$ack in the early 1900s, it is said that Americans would gather on the rooftop of the Gadsden Hotel to watch the fireworks caused by Pancho Villa and his band of desperadoes as they shot their way along the Mexican border. This "Last of the Grand Hotels," located just a mile from the Mexican/American border, has been the center of activity in Douglas since its opening in 1907. Whether the

5:00 A.M. until 9:00 P.M.
Sunday through Wednesday

5:00 A.M. until 10:00 P.M.
Thursday, Friday and Saturday

For reservations
(recommended)
call (520) 364-4481

occasion was watching bandits or entertaining dignitaries, the majestic five-story hotel epitomizes the Old West at its most glamorous.

The hotel, now a National Historic Monument, was named for the Gadsden Purchase of 1853, which granted a section of Mexican territory south of the Gila River to the United States. A fire demolished most of the original hotel building in 1927, but a year later, the hotel was rebuilt with steel and reinforced concrete. The magnificent lobby reflects the opulence of the period. It features vaulted stained-glass skylights, a curving white marble staircase, soaring marble columns topped in fourteen-karat gold leaf, and a stunning forty-two-foot mural made of Tiffany stained glass.

Scores of dignitaries and celebrities stayed at the splendid hotel, including such notables as Eleanor Roosevelt, Charles Lindbergh, Amelia Earhart, Alan Ladd, Paul Newman, and every governor of Arizona. With her glamorous past and old-world grandeur, it's easy to understand why the Gadsaen Hotel is a favorite setting for filmmakers.

When you enter the dining room, located to the left of the lobby, you'll feel as if you've crossed the border into old Mexico. After taking in the wall murals, dark woodwork, and black-leather chairs studded with silver, I half expected to see the likes of the Cisco Kid sitting at one of the tables. He would have felt comfortable in this setting, where everyone seemed to be speaking Spanish and dining on Mexican fare.

I arrived at the restaurant in late morning and was handed both a breakfast menu and one listing lunch and dinner items. Most of the selections were a mix of traditional American and Mexican dishes, and I was in the mood for something a little different. As soon as I spotted the Trail Mix on the breakfast menu, my curiosity was aroused and my decision made.

The platter of food that was placed in front of me could have fueled a band of desperadoes for another round of battle. A hefty mound of creamy refried beans and not-too-hot salsa occupied one side of the plate, and a mound of eggs mixed with tortilla strips, chunks of chorizo, tomatoes, chilies, and cheese filled the other. The whole concoction resembled a loosely held together frittata and was accompanied by a fresh, warm flour tortilla ready to spread with butter. The clean plate proved that everything passed my taste test with flying colors.

Still not ready to hit the trail, I indulged in a piece of Wonderful Cake, one of the restaurant's special desserts. The delightfully moist cake frosted with whipped cream, mandarin oranges, and pineapple, does a wonderful job of soothing the palate after some of the spicier dishes on the menu. Too bad this dessert wasn't around to cool the spurs of Pancho Villa, who reportedly rode his horse up the lobby's marble staircase in 1912, leaving a nasty nick in his wake.

Gadsden Hotel Dining Room's Trail Mix

3 to 4 tablespoons oil
6 corn tortillas, cut into
*   small strips*
½ pound chorizo sausage or
*   chopped ham, cooked and*
*   drained*
1 cup green onions, diced

1 cup tomatoes, diced
1 can green chilies, diced
8 eggs, beaten
½ pound American or
*   cheddar cheese, shredded*
1 cup commercial salsa

Heat oil in large skillet until hot. Fry tortilla strips in oil for 1 to 2 minutes. Add cooked sausage or ham, onions, tomatoes, and chilies. Stir and mix well. Add eggs and cheese and continue stirring and tossing mixture until eggs are set and cheese is melted. Mound into 4 plates and serve with salsa. Serves 4.

Gadsden Hotel Dining Room's Wonderful Cake

1 package (2-layer size)
  yellow cake mix
1 can (11 ounces)
  mandarin oranges in syrup
1 can (8 ounces) crushed
  pineapple
3 eggs
1½ teaspoons vanilla

¾ cup water
¼ cup oil
8 ounces whipping cream
1 small package (3½ ounces)
  vanilla pudding mix
maraschino cherries
  for garnish

Empty cake mix into large mixing bowl. Drain mandarin oranges and crushed pineapple and reserve liquid. Combine fruit liquid. Measure reserved fruit liquid to make ¾ cup and add to cake mix. Add eggs, vanilla, water, and oil. Mix at low speed until ingredients are moistened, then turn mixer to high speed and beat for 2 minutes. Pour batter into prepared 9- by 13-inch baking dish. Bake in 350-degree oven for 35 minutes. Set aside to cool.

Whip whipping cream until stiff. Add vanilla pudding mix to whipped cream a little at a time using gentle, folding movements until pudding is blended into whipped cream. Set aside some mandarin oranges for garnish. Add pineapple and oranges to whipped-cream mixture and fold gently until blended. Frost cooled cake with whipped-cream mixture and decorate with reserved mandarin oranges and maraschino cherries. Makes 1 cake.

Index

Rainbow's End Steakhouse and
Saloon 28

Pies:
Old-Fashioned Chocolate Cream
Pie, Blue Ribbon Cafe 140
Rhubarb Pie, The Nellie Cashman
Restaurant 192

Entrées
Egg Dishes:
Southwestern Eggs, El Tovar
Dining Room 7
Southwestern Quiche, The Garden
Cafe 148
Trail Mix, Gadsden Hotel Dining
Room 199

Fowl:
Blue Corn Chicken Enchiladas,
Macayo's Depot Cantina 115
Capered Chicken, Goldie's 1895
House 91
Chicken and Dumplings, Blue
Ribbon Cafe 139
Chicken Breast with Lemon Butter
Sauce, Samaniego Place Grill
and Bar 172
Chicken Hunter Style, Historic
Saginaw House Restaurant 24
Chicken Morengo, Bella Union
187
Combination Fajitas, Carlos
Murphy's 159
El Presidio Chicken Croquettes,
Janos 168
Garlic Chicken, Willow Creek
Restaurant 52
Lemon Pepper Chicken with
Artichoke Hearts, The Paradise
Bar and Grill 128

Pechuga de Pollo, Aunt Chilada's
at Squaw Peak 83
Pyracantha Chicken, Historic
Saxon House 183
Roast Pheasant Smitane, Charlie
Clark's Steak House 56
Skillet-Seared Breast of Pheasant,
Orangerie at the Arizona
Biltmore 99
Smoked Quail, Arizona Inn 156
Southwestern Chile-Stuffed
Chicken Breast, Dining Car
Cafe 36
Stuffed Duck Legs with Polenta,
Chez Marc Bistro 15

Meat:
Barbecued Ribs, Reata Pass
Steakhouse 71
Beef Strogonaff, El Chorro Lodge
79
Black Peppercorn Steak, Willow
Creek Restaurant 52
Carne Adovada, Los Dos Molinos
95
Chilie-Stuffed New York Steak,
Rainbow's End Steakhouse and
Saloon 27
Combination Fajitas, Carlos
Murphy's 159
Fry Bread Tacos, Bright Angel
Lodge Dining Room 3
Lamb Chops with Rosemary-Port
Sauce, Dining Car Cafe 35
Machaca, El Charro Cafe 163
Medallions of Venison Loin with
Cherry Sauce and Lentil
Ragout, The Terrace Dining
Room at the Wigwam Resort
104
Pork Roast with Brandy Sauce,

Espinaca Con Queso, The Jerome
Grille 32
Green Chile Sauce, Macayo's
Depot Cantina 116
Polenta, Chez Marc Bistro 16
Ranchero Sauce, 1912 136
Red Chile Sauce, Los Olivos
Mexican Patio 68
Roquefort Dressing, Monti's La
Casa Vieja 124
Salsa, Li'l Abner's Steakhouse 151
Smitane Sauce, Charlie Clark's
Steak House 56
Smoked Corn Relish, Bright Angel
Lodge Dining Room 4
Tomatillo Salsa Verde, Copper
Queen Hotel Dining Room 196

Sandwiches

Salmon Burgers, Murphy's 44
Southwestern-Style Grilled
Chicken Sandwich, Samaneigo
Place Grill and Bar 171

Soups and Stews

Black Bean Soup, The Terrace
Dining Room at the Wigwam
Resort 103

Buffalo Chili, Rusty Spur Saloon
and Cafe 75
Chilled Gazpacho Soup, The Tack
Room 175
Clam Chowder, Mill Landing
Restaurant 119
Creamy Corn Chowder, Gurley St.
Grill 39
Green Chile, Los Dos Molinos 96
Southwestern French Onion Soup,
Copper Queen Hotel Dining
Room 195
Tortilla Soup, The Garden Cafe
147
Tortilla Soup, Murphy's 43

Vegetables

Barbecued Beans, Reata Pass
Steakhouse 72
Mexican Rice, Los Olivos Mexi-
can Patio 67
Sonora Enchiladas, Los Olivos
Mexican Patio 68